I0804544

GOD's DIVINE PLAN to BUILD HIS KINGDOM

Learning to Live as God Planned

Roy David Chaney

bookVillages

God's Divine Plan to Build His Kingdom: Learning to Live as God Planned

Not all of the views of the author are necessarily held by the publisher.

ISBN: 978-1-93851-268-1

Cover and interior design by Niddy Griddy Design, Inc.

LCCN: 2022908407

Printed in the United States of America
2 3 4 5 6 7 8 9 10 Printing/Year 26 25 24 23 22

Roy Chaney has delivered a great book from his heart. The big picture of God's kingdom is something that is often overlooked or underrated. This book digs into this with passion and study. Seeing the dynamic of spiritual warfare and God's amazing grace and power in our lives keeps us focused on serving Jesus in a daily powerful way. I enjoyed reading this and hearing Roy on every page. *God's Divine Plan to Build His Kingdom* is a great read for everyone.

Dr. Scott T. Bottoms
Lead Pastor
Church at Briargate

Roy Chaney has a deep desire for the church to arise to the fullness of her destiny. This book is written with great conviction that understanding your role in Jesus's kingdom will enhance the possibilities for this to happen. His discernment of the deeper concepts of the Word will give you strength—and a road map—to follow the standards of God. Looking for knowledge . . . you will certainly find it!

Lana Heightley
Founder and President
Women With A Mission

God's Divine Plan to Build His Kingdom was a real eye-opener for me. It gave me a better perspective on what is going on around me and a better way to deal with it. Everyone knows God has a plan for us, but I think few realize or recognize what Satan is doing to destroy that plan. The book really woke me up from a lax attitude about my relationship with God and heightened my awareness of Satan and his influence around me. I'm not much of a reader and don't read as much as I should, but I couldn't put this book down.

Steve O'Grady

After reading this book, I felt I had a much better understanding of the book of Revelation and what God's plan is for the world and myself personally. It was like reading *Revelation for Dummies,* though it is not dumbed down by any means. I was personally challenged to take responsibility for the free will God has given me to make the decision to truly follow him or try and do things on my own my own way. I learned so much from this book, I recommended and gifted it to several friends and family members.

Paul Reeck

I have been a Christian for most of my life. I have read the Bible, books about it, and studied in church. Roy David Chaney's book *God's Divine Plan to Build His Kingdom: Learning to Live as God Planned* is a must-read for any Christian. I learned about things that I had not understood before. It is written so that you start to think about the Scriptures and what they teach you about God and his plan. Step-by-step it is laid out for you. I love the way Roy brings a thought to you, then backs it up with Scriptures, then explains it so you can understand what has been brought to you. The book is well written and keeps you wanting to read more. Very inspiring! Thank you!

Tanya Wilson

Contents

What Was God's Divine Plan Before the Foundation of the World?

During my study of God's Word, the Holy Spirit has given me divine revelation of God's plan for his creation. However, the more the Holy Spirit has revealed, the more I realize how much I still do not know or understand about God's *entire* plan. My desire is that the Holy Spirit continues revealing to me a deeper understanding of God's intentions to build and expand his kingdom. The following pages express what I believe he has shown me so far.

God's Word is the final authority on truth. *So, what is truth?*

> *All Scripture is inspired by God and is useful to teach us what is true and to make us realize what is wrong in our lives. It corrects us when we are wrong and teaches us to do what is right. God uses it to prepare and equip his people to do every good work.*
> (2 Timothy 3:16–17)

Whenever possible, I will attempt to emphasize the personal relationship that God has with you as a believer in Jesus Christ. Throughout your life, you will choose whom you will serve. When any of us alter the truth of God's Word in our hearts and minds, it changes the truth into a believable lie, and that is dangerous to our spiritual life.

Now let us discover what the Word of God says about his plan. As we study this topic together, my prayer is that we will allow the Holy Spirit to give us his divine revelation of God's Word and open our hearts and minds to what he wants us to fully understand.

The LORD our God has secrets known to no one. Coming to terms with that can save you a lot of frustration. We are not accountable for what he has not shown us, but we and our children will give an account for what we've done with all that he has made plain to us *so that we may obey all the terms of these instructions* (Deuteronomy 29:29). God has revealed more than enough for us to act on to advance his kingdom.

Throughout this study, anytime I talk about God, it is through the perspective of the Trinity: the Father, the Son, and the Holy Spirit. With this in mind, this study presents my perspective on the following questions, based on Scripture:

- What is God's purpose and plan for all his creation?
- Do we understand God's foreknowledge of all things?
- How does this foreknowledge affect God's plan for his eventual kingdom?
- How do Lucifer's decisions impact God's overall plan?
- Why would God decide to put the Tree of the Knowledge of Good and Evil in the garden?
- Why would God allow Lucifer to tempt Adam and Eve, and not just destroy him before he tempted them?
- How important is the Word of God to all of his creation?
- Do we understand the love of God?
- Do we understand the importance of our relationship to Jesus Christ?
- Do we understand the importance of our relationship to the Holy Spirit?
- How do we fit into God's master plan for his kingdom?

We will study God's plan for his creation in these four main sections:

- The Trinity's Plan (the crucifixion of Jesus Christ on the cross)
- Lucifer's Decision
- The Plan for Human Beings
- Jesus Christ Rules for One Thousand Years

You are about to embark on a journey to discover how much God the Father, Jesus Christ the Son, and the Holy Spirit the Advocate loves you, their creation. Following are just some of the truths that you will learn in this study:

- You will learn the importance of loving Jesus Christ with all your heart, mind, and soul.
- You will discover the role the Holy Spirit has in your life and thinking.
- You will learn that you are being created anew, so you can accomplish their plan in your life.
- You will discover the power that has been given to you to be an overcomer of Satan's lies.
- You will learn Satan's true goal for all humanity.
- You will discover how much the Trinity wants their creation to love and obey them with their own free will.
- You will learn how important your role is in building his kingdom with the power that he gives you.
- You will learn how important it is to repent when you stumble and fall.

SECTION 1

The Trinity's Plan

1

Understanding the Plan That Was Established Before the Foundation of the World

We need to remember that the Godhead (the Father, the Son, and the Holy Spirit) are always in agreement in their objective, yet have different responsibilities to accomplish this objective. The three are one, but distinct in function.

The goal in this chapter is to establish that God had a plan to build his kingdom long before the creation of the world. We should not lose sight that God is a creator and his plans will be accomplished throughout eternity. These plans will be introduced in stages, at the appropriate time, by God the Father. This idea is confirmed by Jesus, *"No one knows the day or the hour when these things will happen, not even the angels in heaven or the Son himself. Only the Father knows"* (Matthew 24:36).

In this chapter, we will look at God's decision to create human beings and how that decision would impact the angels, especially in light of what they didn't know at the time.

All of God's creation has been given laws/rules, boundaries/limitations, requirements, and responsibilities to accomplish by his power. But all of God's creation has had trouble understanding what he wanted, and that is why God implemented the next phase of his plan: to create human beings.

That decision set in motion the next objective, which was to reveal to all of his creation who he is. God's plan would be implemented in phases, or in the "*fulness of times*" (Ephesians 1:10, KJV).

As God builds his kingdom, he reveals more and more about himself to all his creation. Mankind is God's greatest creation to date. Through human beings, God is revealing to all his creation his love and his desire to be loved; his holiness, wisdom, and judgment; his presence as our helper; his rulership/leadership, omniscience, authority, righteousness, and creative power; and his mercy, forgiveness, long-suffering kindness, and power. He is showing all of creation that he is a Giver, Teacher, Guide, and Dispenser of grace, joy, hope, character, justice, and redemption. He is mighty, the only Healer, the Alpha and Omega, omnipotent, omnipresent—the list can go on and on.

> *It was to us that God revealed these things by his Spirit. For his Spirit searches out everything and shows us God's deep secrets.* (1 Corinthians 2:10)

Through the Holy Spirit, God revealed to mankind things that had been kept secret since before the six days of creation in Genesis 1–2, and he revealed them only at the appropriate times.

> *Ever since the world was created, people have seen the earth and sky. Through everything God made, they can clearly see his invisible qualities—his eternal power and divine nature. So they have no excuse for not knowing God.* (Romans 1:20)

Have you ever considered that many of God's qualities and attributes were invisible, or at least unknown, to angels before human beings were created? When you think about it, it was never necessary for many of God's attributes to be exhibited to his creation, such as the depth of his love, mercy, forgiveness, and compassion—just to name a few.

God is also revealing that no other created being can possess all of these attributes in their purest form. Therefore, God must be worshipped by his creation as the only true God, with all wisdom and knowledge. His statutes/laws are the only way to live and by which we can be effectively governed.

Another way God reveals himself to mankind is through the Word of God. As we examine his Word throughout this book, we will discover the purpose of free will, and what role the knowledge of good and evil has in God's plan for his creation. We will also discuss what it means to serve an all-knowing God. In addition, we will look at future events. As we begin, let's start by considering the "fullness of time" events.

The following are some of the "fullness of time" events that have already occurred and are going to occur:

Fulfilled:

- Creation before the angels
- Creation of angels
- Creation of human beings
- Lucifer's rebellion
- Adam and Eve's rebellion
- God's covenant with Abraham and his seed
- Jesus Christ given a human body
- The death and resurrection of Jesus Christ
- The outpouring of the Holy Spirit and him living in believers

Future:

- The catching away of the body of Christ
- The Bema seat judgment of the body of Christ and the marriage supper of the Lamb
- Satan's seven-year rule of the world (the tribulation)
- The binding and thousand-year imprisonment of Satan in the bottomless pit
- The thousand-year reign of Jesus Christ, without the influence of Satan
- Satan's short-term release from the bottomless pit to once again deceive the nations
- The great white throne judgment
- The destruction of the old heaven and earth
- The appearance of the new heaven, new earth, and New Jerusalem
- The rule of the body of Christ under Jesus Christ's eternal reign

God is also proving to all of his creation that the only way a kingdom can survive is for all the inhabitants to submit to the authority and laws of their Creator.

This does not come without a great cost to the Godhead and his creation.

More will be discussed in chapter 3 ("Evaluating the Cost").

2

What Is Free Will from God's Perspective?

From the beginning of time, God wanted all his creation to freely choose to worship him, to willingly and voluntarily love him, and to obey his laws and statutes. At the same time, it was necessary for his creation to recognize that they must do all that God requires them to do, under all circumstances, to accomplish the purpose for which they were created.

> *Now I call on heaven and earth to witness the choice you make. Oh, that you would choose life, so that you and your descendants might live! You can make this choice by loving the LORD your God, obeying him, and committing yourself firmly to him. This is the key to your life.* (Deuteronomy 30:19–20)

Let's examine God's purpose for his creation to have free will and the knowledge of good and evil—and how it benefits God's ultimate plan for his kingdom. Angels were created with free will, and they were obedient to the will of God until the next "fullness of time" event occurred. The declaration to angels that God would create human beings, and that the angels would be servant-spirits sent to care for people who will inherit salvation, caused many of them to reevaluate their duties and responsibilities to God. We will discuss the angels' reaction to this revelation further when we study Lucifer/Satan in chapter 9.

> *Angels are only servants—spirits sent to care for people who will inherit salvation.* (Hebrews 1:14)

We must always remember that God is outside of time and is able to see all the choices his creation will make. That does not mean God's creation was created or predestined to sin! That is why all of his creation must be tested and tried, even though God already knows beforehand whom each being will choose to serve. It is necessary that their decisions and consequential actions occur before they can be judged. That way, all of God's creation will see that he judges righteously, based on the choices that people make of their own free will. Your actions are the proof of the decisions you've made and will make.

Since God already knew the unique decisions of each of his angels, he established a plan before the foundation of the world to demonstrate his love to his creation—despite the rebellion of some of the heavenly creatures. However, God's decision would come at a high price, both to the Godhead and to his creation.

> *God paid a ransom to save you from the empty life you inherited from your ancestors. And it was not paid with mere gold or silver, which lose their value. It was the precious blood of Christ, the sinless, spotless Lamb of God. God chose him as your ransom long before the world began, but now in these last days he has been revealed for your sake.* (1 Peter 1:18–20)

The big question for you is this: Have you determined who you are going to serve—God or Lucifer? The decision must be made every day. What will that decision cost you? We will answer that question in the next chapter.

3

Evaluating the Cost

In this chapter, we will look at the Scriptures from two perspectives:

1. God's perspective in building his kingdom
2. God's admonition to human beings who want to be his disciples

> *"If you want to be my disciple, you must, by comparison, hate everyone else—your father and mother, wife and children, brothers and sisters—yes, even your own life. Otherwise, you cannot be my disciple."* (Luke 14:26)

God's decision to proceed with building his kingdom was made before the world was created. God knew that more than one-third of the angels would rebel against his plan and become his enemies. He also knew that in time most of the human race would reject him and become servants of Satan, and that this fallen angel would be their god. So, in the verse above, God was establishing for all his creation that anyone rebelling against his will would become his enemy.

God knew what it would take for human beings to be disciples. Once a person is reconciled with God through the atoning work of Christ, that person should then love God with all of his or her heart, mind, and soul. Your objective as a believer is to obey the leading of the Holy Spirit above all others, even yourself. Do you want to be a disciple of Jesus Christ, willing to follow his lead in all things? Jesus Christ set his standard for being a disciple, and there is simply no deviation from it:

> *"And if you do not carry your own cross and follow me, you cannot be my disciple."* (Luke 14:27)

From this passage we learn that God the Father, Jesus Christ the Son, and the Holy Spirit would have to bear their own cross because of the love they have for God's creation. This would have to happen for them to be successful in building their kingdom. We all know that Jesus Christ died on the cross and shed his blood and rose again for us. However, have we ever considered the anguish and spiritual pain that we cause the Holy Spirit when we refuse to obey his leading? After all, the Holy Spirit lives inside you, giving you counsel and direction on the way to live. To rebel, reject, or defy his direction has consequences far beyond this world.

Now let's consider the cross that God bears for his creation.

God reached a point in Genesis 6:6 that his heart was broken because of the human wickedness on the earth. God had to execute judgment on all the earth because they refused to heed Noah's warning to repent and turn from their evil ways. Their thoughts were only set on evil—continuously! But God's desire and plan to have a creation who would love and obey him will be accomplished. And again, this was known before the foundation of the world.

For the person who wants to be a disciple of Jesus Christ, the Lord establishes the requirements to remain a disciple. The truth about this journey is that to be like Christ, there is going to be a cross to bear. This path will not be easy because you must follow the leading of Jesus Christ and the Holy Spirit. You must never forget that your adversary, the devil, seeks whom he may devour. He wants to consume your soul. What a sad situation for the person who begins this race, and then changes his mind about following the leading of the Holy Spirit and living a holy life.

> *"But don't begin until you count the cost. For who would begin construction of a building without first calculating the cost to see if there is enough money to finish it?"* (Luke 14:28)

This is a probing question. Throughout Scripture, God is building a kingdom, and that cannot be denied. So, when God created Adam and Eve, he had already calculated the cost and determined that their plan would come at a high price. I believe that from God's perspective, the money needed to complete a construction project can be used as an analogy for God's love for his creation. Does God have enough love for his creation to finish their plan? God has declared that he is love and that the work that they began will be completed!

When you accepted Jesus Christ as your personal Savior, you made a decision that you are going to love God with all your heart, mind, and soul (Matthew 22:37). You were also ready to obey what the Holy Spirit says to you, because those decisions will change the direction of your whole life. The way you think, the way you talk, your attitude, even what you do or where you go will be altered. Your life is like a building under construction, and you become an active participant in building the kingdom of God by obeying the Word of God. This decision means that you will no longer believe and do what Lucifer or his advocates say is required of you. The Holy Spirit and God's Word become your authority for the way you live. *So, what is the cost to you? Will you be able to finish your building?* I do believe many fail miserably in teaching this part of the Word of God!

> *"Otherwise, you might complete only the foundation before running out of money, and then everyone would laugh at you. They would say, 'There's the person who started that building and couldn't afford to finish it!'"* (Luke 14:29–30)

God the Father, God the Son, and God the Holy Spirit will not run out of love for you, and they will finish the work if you allow them to do it.

The passage above describes people who accept Jesus Christ as their Savior, and Jesus Christ is that foundation, and then, somewhere along their journey, they lose their first love in Jesus Christ. When you first get redeemed (saved), you tell everyone. The way you talk and think, your attitude, and even where you go will begin to change as you start to follow the leading of the Holy Spirit.

But the new lifestyle becomes hard, and you may even not like the change, so you begin to lose your love for Jesus Christ. Now your friends, family, coworkers, and so on will make fun of you and your decision to love God. They will ridicule you and even talk to others about your decision.

How could this happen? I believe that those who experience this did not count the cost, or even understand the changes that would occur in their lives or the peer pressure they would receive. This did not happen because God did not have enough power to complete the work! God will not violate your choice in serving him with all your heart, mind, and soul. You are a free moral agent, and you will choose whom you will serve: God or Lucifer.

> *"Or what king would go to war against another king without first sitting down with his counselors to discuss whether his army of 10,000 could defeat the 20,000 soldiers marching against him?"* (Luke 14:31)

God knew before he created human beings that war was going to occur with fallen angels, and Lucifer would become their king. So, the Godhead evaluated whether or not it was that important for them to build a kingdom of created beings that would worship and obey them only. They also knew that their army would be outnumbered, because most of these human beings would not accept Jesus Christ as Lord or King. Never forget that when people refuse to accept Jesus Christ as their Savior, they become advocates (soldiers) of Lucifer and his army. There is no middle ground here. The day is coming when Jesus Christ will take his rightful place as King of kings and Lord of lords. We are seeing this war happening before our eyes.

Now, as a new believer, you must determine whether you love God enough to go to war with him, to win the lost? You must recognize that many of your friends, coworkers, and family members will become your enemies and will make fun of you and consider you a fool. This does not mean that you hate your enemies; you must love and forgive them (just like Christ did). You do this so that you can influence them to accept Jesus Christ as their Savior. The battle that is raging is energized by Satan's influence on those who oppose Christ. So, counting the cost is an evaluation that you must make, not just for today, but for the rest of your life.

> *For God bought you with a high price. So you must honor God with your body.* (1 Corinthians 6:20)

This verse reinforces the price God paid for you— while declaring what God requires of you, to honor him with your body.

> *God paid a high price for you, so don't be enslaved by the world.* (1 Corinthians 7:23)

This verse establishes the possibility that you can once again become enslaved by the world (Satan's influence).

4

The Mystery of God's Plan

There is an aspect of God's plan that is a mystery/secret and is not revealed to his creation until the appropriate time. Why? Because it could alter free will. Because it would give information to the powers of this world that would enable them to alter prophecy! And to prove to God's creation that Christ living in you is the only power that can give you the power to control your free will, to make you fit for his kingdom.

> *Yet when I am among mature believers, I do speak with words of wisdom, but not the kind of wisdom that belongs to this world or to the rulers of this world, who are soon forgotten. No, the wisdom we speak of is the mystery of God—his plan that was previously hidden, even though he made it for our ultimate glory before the world began. But the rulers of this world have not understood it; if they had, they would not have crucified our glorious Lord.* (1 Corinthians 2:6–8)

These verses describe Christians who can speak wisdom given to them by the Holy Spirit, at the right time. If Lucifer knew or understood God's plan, he would have never influenced the fallen angels and the people of this world to crucify Jesus. Therefore, Lucifer must be allowed to have free will, within the limits that God has placed on him. If Lucifer would have known God's plan, he would have altered prophecy, and that would have made God a liar. This passage also establishes the fact that angels and human beings have limited wisdom and understanding.

> *This message was kept secret for centuries and generations past, but now it has been revealed to God's people. For God wanted them to know that the riches and glory of Christ are for you Gentiles, too. And this is the secret: Christ lives in you.* (Colossians 1:26–27)

God will prove to all his creation that worshipping and obeying him is the only way a kingdom can exist without being destroyed. After all, a kingdom divided against itself cannot stand. Do you really understand what it means that Jesus Christ lives in you? With Jesus Christ living in you, you have received all the power you need to break every chain that binds you and holds you in captivity to Satan's influence, so you can be free to live the way God requires you to live in this world!

> *And when he brought his supreme Son into the world, God said, "Let all of God's angels worship him."*
> (Hebrews 1:6)

When this part of God's plan occurred, everything changed for angels and human beings. Now angels would be required to worship God's Son in a new form.

Angels had never seen God's supreme Son in this form before. They also had never seen this kind of love expressed to any of God's creation because it was not necessary before Lucifer's rebellion against the authority of God. God was revealing all of his attributes to all of his creation at the same time.

> *That is why, when Christ came into the world, he said to God, "You did not want animal sacrifices or sin offerings. But you have given me a body to offer."*
> (Hebrews 10:5)

We can see clearly that it was not God's perfect will that any of his creation would rebel against his authority and sin, which would then require animal sacrifices/sin offerings. These animal sacrifices only pushed their sins forward until Jesus Christ could make the ultimate sacrifice for the benefit of human beings, not angels.

God's perfect will wanted all of his creation to worship him as God and submit to his authority in all things forever.

However, God knew before the world was created that his creation, with free will, would rebel against his authority. And so it would be necessary for Christ to offer his body as a sacrifice for (only) human beings, at the appropriate time. Only those human beings who accept Jesus Christ as their Lord and Savior, submit to his authority, and obey will receive eternal life as their reward.

> *We proclaim to you the one who existed from the beginning, whom we have heard and seen. We saw him with our own eyes and touched him with our own hands. He is the Word of life. This one who is life itself was revealed to us, and we have seen him. And now we testify and proclaim to you that he is the one who is eternal life. He was with the Father, and then he was revealed to us.*
> (1 John 1:1–2)

The disciples lacked real understanding of who Jesus Christ was, and what he came to do. And that did not change until after he died and rose again, when they were empowered by the Holy Spirit. This passage also describes how important it was to them that they were able to physically see and touch Jesus. I would like to reveal to you an area of my understanding that is still a mystery to me about the Trinity.

> *No one has ever seen God.* (1 John 4:12)

> *No one has ever seen God. But the unique One, who is himself God, is near to the Father's heart. He has revealed God to us.* (John 1:18)

> *"Not that anyone has ever seen the Father; only I, who was sent from God, have seen him."* (John 6:46)

> *"Anyone who has seen me has seen the Father!"* (John 14:9)

These verses seem to declare that no one in God's creation had ever seen God the Father. We know that before human beings were created, the angels understood the concept of the Trinity because they worshipped God at the throne and said, "Holy, holy, holy," recognizing the presence of the Spirit of the Trinity.

However, my question remains: During that dispensation of time, were the angels ever able to see the Trinity as we understand seeing?

Read Psalm 139. There, David describes God in a profound way. Yet God knows you the same way, along with every believer. My mind cannot comprehend the kind of love, power, and ability that God has for his creation. Also, how can the Holy Spirit live in each of us at the same time? And yet he is able to give us counsel and power from Jesus Christ so we can be overcomers of Satan's influence—all because of their love for each of us, and all of this happens in each of our lives at the same time.

> *Without question, this is the great mystery of our faith: Christ was revealed in a human body and vindicated by the Spirit. He was seen by angels and announced to the nations. He was believed in throughout the world and taken to heaven in glory.* (1 Timothy 3:16)

This verse seems to indicate that angels were not able to see the Son of God until he was given a human body. Second, the announcement to the nations was to the angelic world. At that time they understood and recognized that Jesus Christ was the Son of God their Creator. This was accomplished because Jesus Christ was without sin. Jesus was obedient to God in all that was required of him to do and accomplish. All angels, heavenly and fallen, believed in the deity of Jesus Christ.

Please consider this: Satan understood the importance for God's creation to worship God. That is why he influenced and led human beings to create idols or other gods to worship. The need to worship God was already built into the minds and hearts of human beings. However, they refused to worship a God they could not physically see and touch. Remember when the Jews built the golden calf? This need to physically see the god they were going to worship made them chase after idols, and this happened over and over again.

> *Christ is the visible image of the invisible God. He existed before anything was created and is supreme over all creation.* (Colossians 1:15)

This verse describes Jesus Christ in a different state of existence. Jesus can now be seen by his creation and stated that when you see him, you have seen God. You are able to physically see the characteristics of God through Jesus Christ.

> *Oh, how great are God's riches and wisdom and knowledge! How impossible it is for us to understand his decisions and his ways! For who can know the LORD's thoughts? Who knows enough to give him advice? And who has given him so much that he needs to pay it back? For everything comes from him and exists by his power and is intended for his glory. All glory to him forever!* (Romans 11:33–36)

Many mysteries have already been revealed, and now we can understand them. However, some mysteries are yet to be revealed. Are you willing to allow the Holy Spirit to reveal the mysteries yet to come in your life? Are you listening to what the Holy Spirit is saying to you?

> *When the seventh angel blows his trumpet, God's mysterious plan will be fulfilled. It will happen just as he announced it to his servants the prophets.* (Revelation 10:7)

That day is coming! Where will you spend eternity?

5

Understanding God's Plan and His Part in Building His Kingdom

It is important to understand that since God exists outside of time, he knew that Lucifer would rebel against his plan for this new creation (human beings). Because of the love and desire the Godhead had for this new creation, the Father, Son, and Spirit determined what would be necessary to redeem fallen humanity. God established the responsibility each person of the Godhead would have in this redemption process. It was also determined what role each person (in the body of Christ) would have in building the kingdom of God. They would be given everything they need to accomplish their calling. This plan was established before the foundation of the world. God would determine the exact time when every aspect of the plan would be implemented.

> *"The Father alone has the authority to set those dates and times, and they are not for you to know."* (Acts 1:7)

God himself determines when each transition of time is executed. This reminder by Jesus also tells us that God has determined that none of his creation will know these dates or times when the transition of events will occur.

> *But God knew what would happen, and his prearranged plan was carried out when Jesus was betrayed.* (Acts 2:23)

Before the world was created, God knew what would be required to redeem mankind as a result of their rebellion to his authority. God also knew the influence that Satan and the fallen angels would have on mankind. God's plan began when Jesus was betrayed by mankind, just as God was betrayed by Lucifer/Satan, because it set off the next chain of events of Jesus Christ's death and resurrection for the sins of mankind.

> *It is God alone who judges.* (Psalm 75:7)

Judgment is determined by God for all of his creation throughout eternity.

Ezekiel 18:4 says, *"For all people are mine to judge—both parents and children alike. And this is my rule: The person who sins is the one who will die."* I believe the word *die* here means separation from God, not just physical death. God is the judge.

> *For we are God's masterpiece. He has created us anew in Christ Jesus, so we can do the good things he planned for us long ago.* (Ephesians 2:10)

You are God's masterpiece. When you accept Jesus Christ as your personal Savior, you are created anew in Christ and given spiritual gifts to advance God's kingdom. Satan's power over you is broken; you now have the power to do the good things God called you to do before you were created.

> *For God's gifts and his call can never be withdrawn.* (Romans 11:29)

God has given you gifts and talents, and you are called to accomplish the things he has called you to do. You will never be able to accuse God of giving you the wrong gift or talent. You will choose if you are going to be obedient to your call and use the gift and talent for the glory of God. When you stand before God at your judgment time, he will never say to you, "I made a mistake."

> *For God is love.* (1 John 4:8)

More will be discussed about God's love in chapter 6.

6

Understanding God's Plan and Jesus Christ's Role in Building the Kingdom

> *For you know that God paid a ransom to save you from the empty life you inherited from your ancestors. And it was not paid with mere gold or silver, which lose their value. It was the precious blood of Christ, the sinless, spotless Lamb of God. God chose him as your ransom long before the world began, but now in these last days he has been revealed for your sake.*
>
> —1 Peter 1:18–20

The ultimate evidence of God's love for you is when the Father decided it was time to give his Son, Jesus, a body so it could be sacrificed for you. His blood would cover the sins of those human beings who accept Jesus and begin to obey him. This transaction is the only way to overcome the power of Satan over human beings—and all of this was known by God before the world began.

> *This is real love—not that we loved God, but that he loved us and sent his Son as a sacrifice to take away our sins.* (1 John 4:10)

This verse establishes what real love is. All human beings were sinners who did not love God because they were willingly controlled by the influence of Satan. Because of Jesus Christ's sacrifice, our past sins can be forgiven and we can receive power to overcome the influence of Satan. And so, we don't have to sin anymore. If you sin, all you have to do is repent and obey what the Holy Spirit tells you to do.

> *But when the right time came, God sent his Son, born of a woman, subject to the law.* (Galatians 4:4)

This verse establishes that God determined the time when his Son would be born of a woman, which would make Jesus subject to the law of God, just as all human beings are subject to God's law.

> *God qualified him [Jesus Christ] as a perfect High Priest.* (Hebrews 5:9)

God established that Jesus Christ was the only sacrifice that he would accept and so he became your High Priest for the forgiveness of sins.

> *For by that one offering he forever made perfect those who are being made holy. And the Holy Spirit also testifies that this is so. For he says, "This is the new covenant I will make with my people on that day, says the LORD: I will put my laws in their hearts, and I will write them on their minds."* (Hebrews 10:14–16)

This passage establishes that Jesus Christ is the one and only sacrifice that would take the place of all the animal sacrifices God's chosen people had to make to him. It also states that when you commit your life to Jesus Christ, something profound begins to happen. A new covenant is established with you, one that places the laws of God in your heart and writes them on your mind. Now you no longer can make the claim "I didn't know that was sin." The Holy Spirit begins his work in your life to make you holy. As the Holy Spirit reveals what is wrong in your heart and soul, you begin to change because you love God and want to be like Jesus. Do you realize that after you die a physical death and stand before God's judgment throne, the Holy Spirit will be your witness that you repented of your sin and became more like Christ?

> *This means that anyone who belongs to Christ has become a new person. The old life is gone; a new life has begun!* (2 Corinthians 5:17)

This verse states that when you belong to Christ, the way you once lived your life is now gone. You will begin to think, speak, and walk differently. A transformation begins in your life. Your life now gives glory to God, to everyone with whom you come in contact, by the power of Jesus Christ. Wow, what a change!

> *But the Son of God came to destroy the works of the devil.* (1 John 3:8)

From the moment Adam and Eve gave in to Satan's temptation, all human beings (Adam and Eve's genetic descendants) received Satan's DNA to lie and rebel against God's authority, his law, and his Word. Now Jesus Christ has come to destroy the devil's work (DNA) in your body and soul—if you will let him. Now you're in Christ and have the power to overcome Satan's influence.

> *The Son also became flesh and blood. For only as a human being could he die, and only by dying could he break the power of the devil, who had the power of death.* (Hebrews 2:14)

Again, Adam and Eve sinned in the garden, and now all human beings are under the judgment of God because they disobeyed God's commands. Lucifer had the power of death over all human beings from that time forward. That death is physical and spiritual. Once Adam and Eve fell, their descendants would not live forever, and they would be under the control of Satan and separated from God.

However, God had already established a plan to redeem human beings. That would require the Son of God (in a human body) to be tempted by Lucifer. This meant that Jesus Christ would have to be obedient to God and his plan, in every way, and live without sin.

Once that was complete, Jesus Christ would have to die to redeem human beings from their sin and give them power to be overcomers. Then the devil's power of death over human beings would be broken. Now, human beings can choose to serve, obey, and worship God—and they can make that decision for themselves. However, that is only accomplished through the power of Jesus Christ.

The reason human beings will go to hell is because they refuse to believe in Jesus Christ or acknowledge their sinfulness before him. Jesus is the only One who can change the way you think. Because of his power in you, your actions in life can be totally different—if you obey. If only human beings would believe and obey God their Creator! What a different world we could live in!

Jesus Christ will rule human beings, along with the bride of Christ, for one thousand years, without the influence of Lucifer, who will be in the bottomless pit during that time.

7

Understanding God's Plan and the Holy Spirit's Role in Building the Kingdom

> *The Spirit of God, who raised Jesus from the dead, lives in you. And just as God raised Christ Jesus from the dead, he will give life to your mortal bodies by this same Spirit living within you.*
>
> —Romans 8:11

The verse above declares that the Holy Spirit raised Jesus from the dead and that that same Spirit lives in you. Yet, Satan's lie that the Holy Spirit has no place in today's society, and therefore he does not live in you (the Christian), can be compelling. What damage that has caused in the lives of professing Christians! Do you recognize the Holy Spirit in your life? This verse also reminds us that the Holy Spirit will raise your dead mortal body up from the grave at the appropriate time.

> *Because the Spirit who lives in you is greater than the spirit who lives in the world.* (1 John 4:4)

This verse declares that the Holy Spirit in you is greater, more powerful, than the spirit of the Antichrist. However, you are the only one who determines if you are going to believe the Word of God.

> *And God has given us his Spirit as proof that we live in him and he in us.* (1 John 4:13)

Do you need more evidence that God loves you? Will you love God with all your heart, mind, and soul?

> *"But in fact, it is best for you that I go away, because if I don't, the Advocate won't come. If I do go away, then I will send him to you. And when he comes, he will convict the world of its sin, and of God's righteousness, and of the coming judgment. The world's sin is that it refuses to believe in me."* (John 16:7–9)

Jesus stated that it was for you that he was going away, so the Holy Spirit (the Advocate) can come and live in you, and through you he will convict the world of its sin and declare God's righteousness and the coming judgment. You see, even you are going to stand before God and give an account. If you refuse to believe in Jesus Christ, your sins will never be forgiven at your judgment. By then, it will be too late to believe in Jesus Christ. However, at that time, you will still acknowledge and bow down to the King of kings and Lord of lords. Even so, you will be separated from God in hell for eternity, wishing you had made a different decision when you were given the opportunity.

> *"When the Spirit of truth comes, he will guide you into all truth. He will not speak on his own but will tell you what he has heard. He will tell you about the future. He will bring me glory by telling you whatever he receives from me. All that belongs to the Father is mine; this is why I said, 'The Spirit will tell you whatever he receives from me.'"* (John 16:13–15)

This passage is powerful if you understand and believe it. Jesus declared that when the Spirit comes—which already happened on the day of Pentecost—the Spirit will guide you into all truth. So, once you give your heart and life to Jesus, the Spirit will guide you.

You see, now you already have the Word of God planted into your heart and mind. Jesus Christ will give to the Holy Spirit divine revelation on how you are to apply the Word of God in your life. This is done to give glory to Jesus Christ and to give you what you need, so you can begin to live a holy life.

What happens when you stop obeying what the Holy Spirit tells you to do? You begin the process of searing your own conscience. If this goes on long enough, the destruction of your soul lies at the door. Why? Because you don't want to give up your old lifestyle, and you have decided that you don't love God with all your heart, mind, and soul. After all, you will choose whom you are going to serve—God the Creator or Satan the destroyer. Please, listen and obey what the Holy Spirit says for you to do! Don't give up!

> *But you have received the Holy Spirit, and he lives within you, so you don't need anyone to teach you what is true. For the Spirit teaches you everything you need to know, and what he teaches is true—it is not a lie. So just as he has taught you, remain in fellowship with Christ.* (1 John 2:27)

The Holy Spirit is powerful and effective in teaching you how to live your life—if you will follow his leading. The Holy Spirit will reveal to you the truth about what other people will say to you about God's Word. You can always know that the Holy Spirit is telling you the truth because it will never be in conflict with the Word of God. You must always examine what other people tell you against the Word of God.

> *But the Holy Spirit produces this kind of fruit in our lives: love, joy, peace, patience, kindness, goodness, faithfulness, gentleness, and self-control. There is no law against these things!* (Galatians 5:22–23)

The Bible, God's Word, tells you to examine yourself to see if you are in the faith. So, test yourself! Do you want to know if you are allowing the Holy Spirit to be effective in your life? Do you witness the fruit of love, joy, peace, patience, kindness, goodness, faithfulness, gentleness, and self-control in your life? Do you know that you need to allow the Holy Spirit to continue his work in your life?

The Holy Spirit begins with love, and the progression continues with joy; next, peace, and so on; this is a building process. You see, you will never have self-control without all the other fruit of the Holy Spirit already displayed in your life. You have the ability to stop the Holy Spirit's work in you if refuse to obey his leading. You will choose whom you will serve!

8

God's Divine Plan: Angels Called to Participate in Building the Kingdom of God

When God created angels, he established rules, boundaries, limitations, requirements, and responsibilities for them. God gave them different ranks and responsibilities to accomplish and obey. God created angels with free will!

Angels are spirits who worship God. I believe God called them to care for human beings who will inherit salvation.

I believe that God did not create angels with the characteristic of love as we know it or with the ability to procreate.

Angels were not created in God's own image.

Angels are not gods, nor do they possess the attributes of the Godhead.

No angel can be in more than one place at a time. Angels are invisible to man, most of the time.

I believe angels cannot make or build anything.

> *And furthermore, it is not angels who will control the future world.* (Hebrews 2:5)

This verse establishes that God has determined that angels will never control the future world—and that includes Lucifer. Satan will eventually lose his current residence and title as the prince of the power of the air, along with the rest of the fallen angels.

> *The Son did not come to help angels.* (Hebrews 2:16)

This verse states that Jesus Christ did not come to redeem angels. So, the question I have is, Why not?

> *For it is impossible to bring back to repentance those who were once enlightened—those who have experienced the good things of heaven and shared in the Holy Spirit, who have tasted the goodness of the word of God and the power of the age to come—and who then turn away from God. It is impossible to bring such people back to repentance.* (Hebrews 6:4–6)

I know this verse specifically identifies human beings. However, I believe it also applies to all angels that rebelled against God's command. How can we deny that all angels were not enlightened, were not experienced in the good things of heaven, did not share in God's presence, and did not worship the Godhead? Those who fell had tasted the goodness of the Word of God and then turned away from him! You see, God had given them everything he had, and still many rejected their Creator and authority.

> *But Jesus told him, "Anyone who puts a hand to the plow and then looks back is not fit for the Kingdom of God."* (Luke 9:62)

I believe this verse also applies to angels who chose their own free will over the will of God.

We will discuss both of these verses later in another chapter as it relates to human beings.

Ever since Adam and Eve disobeyed God, evil angels have had access to the minds of human beings. While they cannot read our minds, they can introduce thoughts into them. Their mission is to get human beings to disobey God's laws for their ultimate destruction.

Let's look at more evidence that angels have free will, especially to fulfill God's commission to help human beings. It appears that all angels are being tested and tried to see if they will be obedient to God's authority and command so as not to fall into darkness and be chained into prisons of darkness as stated in Jude 6.

> *And I remind you of the angels who did not stay within the limits of authority God gave them but left the place where they belonged. God has kept them securely chained in prisons of darkness, waiting for the great day of judgment.*

This Scripture highlights four important points:

1. It is apparent that these angels were not among the angels who fell with Lucifer in the beginning.
2. There is no indication of the number of angels that did not obey God's command.
3. I believe these angels went beyond the authority God gave them, namely, to help mankind.
4. This verse describes the consequences for angels who allowed their free will to take over.

SECTION 2

Lucifer's Decision

9

Who Is Lucifer/Satan?

God created Lucifer, perhaps to be the highest-ranking angel in heaven. Did God know Lucifer would rebel against his authority before he created him?

Since God has declared that he is all-knowing, he had to know. Yet he still created Lucifer in beauty, full of wisdom, and gave him a position of authority. I believe when God allowed Lucifer to tempt Adam and Eve to disobey God's command, that is all the proof you need to establish that angels were created with free will.

> *"For you said to yourself, 'I will ascend to heaven and set my throne above God's stars. I will preside on the mountain of the gods far away in the north. I will climb to the highest heavens and be like the Most High.'"*
> (Isaiah 14:13–14)

Lucifer said to himself (not God), *"I will ascend to heaven and set my throne above God's stars."* This establishes that Lucifer was not satisfied with what God had created him to do—he wanted more. He continues with his thought process, *"I will preside on the mountain of the gods . . . [and] climb to the highest heavens."* However, God knows the thoughts of all his creation. I don't believe that Lucifer understood the truth about God's ability to know what created beings were thinking, at least at that time. Lucifer believed in his own mind that he would find a way to be like God and be worshipped as God. Satan eventually even had the audacity to tempt Jesus to worship him.

Lucifer was not satisfied with the position of authority and responsibility that was given to him by God.

> *"Son of man, sing this funeral song for the king of Tyre. Give him this message from the Sovereign Lord: 'You were the model of perfection, full of wisdom and exquisite in beauty. You were in Eden, the garden of God. . . . I ordained and anointed you as the mighty angelic guardian. You had access to the holy mountain of God and walked among the stones of fire. You were blameless in all you did from the day you were created until the day evil was found in you.'"* (Ezekiel 28:12–15)

It is apparent that the king of Tyre is Lucifer, and the Son of Man (Jesus) is given the task of singing this funeral song, given to him by the Sovereign Lord (God). God describes how he created Lucifer, a model of perfection, full of wisdom and exquisite beauty. The whole angelic world was witness to the attributes and responsibility God had given to Lucifer. These verses establish that Lucifer was in Eden, the garden of God, with the responsibility to be a guardian of God's new creation. They also establish that Lucifer had access to the holy mountain of God and walked among the stones of fire, which represented God's holiness.

Before Adam and Eve were created, God revealed a mystery to all the angels, that they would be given another responsibility:

> *Therefore, angels are only servants—spirits sent to care for people who will inherit salvation.* (Hebrews 1:14)

God's decision and revelation to the angels, namely, that it was time to create human beings in God's own image to rule the world, was the catalyst that caused Lucifer to question God's decision to let human beings have dominion over the world—instead of him (Lucifer). Lucifer's reaction to God's decision did not catch the Lord by surprise. Now what was Lucifer going to do? Was he going to rule over his thought process or rebel against God's authority?

Did Lucifer have free will and the power to overcome his desire to be like God? Did Lucifer have the same option as Cain?

> *Abel also brought a gift—the best portions of the first-born lambs from his flock. The LORD accepted Abel and his gift.* (Genesis 4:4)

This verse indicates that Adam and Eve and their family knew that an offering of worship to God was required. Abel was obedient to God and his requirements, so Abel was accepted along with his gift.

> *But he did not accept Cain and his gift. This made Cain very angry, and he looked dejected. "Why are you so angry?" the LORD asked Cain. "Why do you look so dejected? You will be accepted if you do what is right. But if you refuse to do what is right, then watch out! Sin is crouching at the door, eager to control you. But you must subdue it and be its master."* (Genesis 4:5–7)

This story describes what occurs when you refuse to obey what God requires of you—all because you want to do it your way. There is no joy or peace in your heart or mind! You actually become angry at God, and you spill out your anger on someone else. When you obey what God requires, you will have joy in your heart and mind, and then others will see the evidence that you have peace with God and others.

So, what is sin? Sin is refusing to obey what God commands and requires of you. This desire to do it your own way comes from Satan's influence on you to reject God's authority to establish laws and requirements on your life. Please, let me make this clear: Satan has no power to make you do anything! There's no such thing as "the devil made me do it"!

Again, you will choose whom you are going to serve. I believe that Lucifer (Satan) wants to control you so you will disobey God and lose your own soul for eternity. After all, Lucifer already knows the outcome of his judgment, and he desires to destroy you as well.

Again, did Lucifer, with free will, have the power to overcome his desire to be like God? Did Lucifer have the same option as Cain?

We know that Lucifer said to himself *I will* many times in his mind. His stated intention to be like the Most High meant that he had evil thoughts and intents in his heart. Then Lucifer actually acted on his plan to convince Adam and Eve to disobey God's law and to refuse to be the guardian angel (to protect God's new creation).

Ever since Lucifer was created, he was blameless and he obeyed God, fulfilling and following through with all of God's requirements. From the day he was created, Lucifer (with his free will) overcame all other thoughts of disobedience to God's commands until this set of events occurred. That is why it is so dangerous for God's creation (with their free will) to entertain thoughts of disobedience to God's laws for long, because it leads you down a path that makes you think that your way is better than God's way.

Another reason that God allowed Lucifer to carry out his dark plan was that all the other angels did not know the thoughts of Lucifer. They would not have understood God's judgment on Lucifer.

When God decided to create human beings, he knew that all of his creation would have to be tested and tried, because he knew what was in the heart and mind of Lucifer. The reason the Tree of the Knowledge of Good and Evil was placed in the garden was to test angels and human beings at the same time. All of God's creation must know and understand the consequences of not obeying God at all times.

> *"He was a murderer from the beginning. He has always hated the truth, because there is no truth in him. When he lies, it is consistent with his character; for he is a liar and the father of lies."* (John 8:44)

Wow. We need to truly understand what Jesus was declaring in this verse. What does it mean when he declared that Lucifer was a murderer from the beginning? When was the beginning? I believe the beginning was when God introduced his plan to the angels that he was going to create human beings in their own image and that they would rule the world. It was that time when Lucifer first hated human beings that made him a murderer. You see, God considers all of his creation his family. Who are we to hate what God has created? Another verse that reveals God's definition of murder is 1 John 3:15:

> *Anyone who hates another brother or sister is really a murderer at heart.*

What was the truth that Lucifer hated? We will eventually discuss another verse that I believe will give us more insight about John 8:44.

> *Jesus told him [Thomas], "I am the way, the truth, and the life."* (John 14:6)

Everything that God is and everything he says is the truth, for God is truth.

We need to examine the rest of John 8:44. The moment that Lucifer executed his plan to become like God and lied to Adam and Eve that it was okay not to obey the command of God not to eat the fruit, *that* was the beginning of a new existence for Lucifer. Everything changed. Lucifer was the guardian angel, the leader of worship in heaven. At that moment of rebellion, a new beginning occurred. Lucifer became Satan, the destroyer, the enemy of God. From that time forward, Satan hated the truth (God) because the personification of truth (God) was no longer in him. Now, for Satan to achieve his goal, his character had to devolve into darkness. So, he had to continue to lie—even to this day. Satan lied to the angels about what God had told him.

> *For God never said to any angel what he said to Jesus: "You are my Son."* (Hebrews 1:5)

Why did it become necessary for God to declare that he never told any angel, "You are my Son"? Jesus was not only the Son of God, but he was given the position of authority and rulership over human beings. Satan told the angels that God had given him the authority to rule over human beings, and approximately one-third of the angels believed this lie. These angels were no longer willing to continue in obedience to God's will or purpose as to why they were created.

This was the first time that any being of God's creation had ever lied to anyone! The last part of John 8:44 declares that Satan is *"the father of lies."* To receive more understanding of what happened, let's look at three words in Ezekiel 28:12. Lucifer was "*full of wisdom*" given to him by God. Of all the angels, Lucifer was given more knowledge (wisdom) about who God is and what God required from his creation, and understood more of God's characteristics. With that knowledge, Satan understood how to get human beings to disobey God by creating lies! Just look at all the false gods that Satan has created. Have we considered 1 Timothy 4:1?

> *They will follow deceptive spirits and teachings that come from demons.*

Will you follow any of these false teachings?

Satan created evolution (the lie) to try to destroy the truth of how God created the world and everything in it, such as, to legalize abortions, to justify killing the unborn.

Satan has given human beings the desire to lie (because his DNA has been in us since the fall), and he has inspired specific individuals to be the authors of these lies to give credibility to humanity that these lies are the truth.

All of these lies and so many more are Satan's strategy to separate you from the love of God so that you will receive the same judgment from God as he will. So, when the Bible says Satan is the father of lies, that means that Satan is the originator of all that is untrue. His only objective is to destroy you, because he now knows that God will never allow him to have a throne and preside on the mountain of God and be like the Most High.

> *And all liars—their fate is in the fiery lake of burning sulfur.* (Revelation 21:8)

Why will God cast all liars into hell? Because Satan's character is a liar, and those who lie have justified their lying to get what they want, just like Satan. That is why the body of Christ should never lie, not even what we call little white lies. Because lying begins the process of changing your character from being Christlike to being more like Satan's deceptive character.

Lucifer challenged God's authority and believed he could do a better job, so rebellion was introduced. This action challenged every aspect of God and who he is. Lucifer's rebellion began to grow against every rule, boundary or limitation, requirement, and responsibility that was given to him.

> *Stay alert! Watch out for your great enemy, the devil. He prowls around like a roaring lion, looking for someone to devour.* (1 Peter 5:8)

This verse establishes the importance of being aware of what is happening around you. It also states that you have a great enemy who is trying to destroy everything that God has planned for you. The passage also establishes your responsibility to follow the lead of the Holy Spirit, because you are the decision-maker of what you do.

Here are some facts about Satan: All angels are created spirits, including Satan, and so they are not omnipresent. They can only be in one place at a time. If Satan is not omnipresent, then how can he influence you? That happens through his DNA, which has been passed down from generation to generation and is present in you at birth.

The same spiritual DNA was passed down to all the angels (demons) that rebelled against God and were cast out of heaven. All the demons follow the orders of Satan, and they have created a strategy to overcome you.

Please don't forget that human beings who are controlled by Satan's influence can be part of his plan to influence you. That is why you must hold fast to the power and truth that you have been given, and never stop following the leading of the Holy Spirit; never give up.

> *"Once again I will shake not only the earth but the heavens also."* (Hebrews 12:26)

This means that all creation will be shaken and removed, so that only unshakable things will remain.

The fact is, God loves you; however, he gave you free will to choose to make your own decisions. Would you worship him and live under his authority and rule, or would you venerate Lucifer and live under his authority and rule? After all, you were created by God, for him! So, in this way, all the angels and all human beings will be tested and tried.

So here is God's big question for you: Whom are you going to serve? Will you obey God, Lucifer, or yourself? The only way that you will be unshakable is for you to remain in Christ Jesus. If you miss the mark and sin, repent from your heart and mind; ask Jesus for the power to overcome Satan's influence. God's power has already been made available to you, all because you love God and he loves you.

> *Today I have given you the choice between life and death, between blessings and curses. Now I call on heaven and earth to witness the choice you make. Oh, that you would choose life, so that you and your descendants might live! You can make this choice by loving the LORD your God, obeying him, and committing yourself firmly to him. This is the key to your life.*
> (Deuteronomy 30:19–20)

Throughout history, God is proving to all his creation that worshipping and obeying him is the only way a kingdom can exist without being destroyed. After all, a kingdom divided against itself cannot stand. At your judgment, there will be witnesses of what you actually did in your lifetime, including the Holy Spirit, Jesus Christ, angels, and human beings, so that all will know that God's judgment concerning you will be fair and just.

So, what is good? Everything about God is good—his ways, his statutes, his laws, his judgments, and his plan. However, we do not fully understand all of God's goodness, and it won't be revealed until the appropriate time. It is way beyond our understanding at this time!

So, what is evil? Evil is when any of God's creations question any part of God's goodness, ways, laws, and judgments or think their way is better than God's way. The next step of evil is when God's creation rebels and will not obey his command. That is when we start seeing the consequences of our rebellion.

Lucifer's claim that he could rule and govern human beings

better than God resulted in a challenge to determine who should rule God's creation. So, God allowed Lucifer to tempt Adam and Eve to see whom they would serve. God determined that this act of rebellion by Lucifer would be the vehicle to test all of his creation.

> *Jesus knew their thoughts and replied, "Any kingdom divided by civil war is doomed. A town or family splintered by feuding will fall apart."* (Matthew 12:25)

Is it really a mystery what is happening in America today? We are witnessing rebellion against authority, rebellion against God's law and his Word, the inability and unwillingness to forgive, and the type of hatred that dominates our society. The only way America can survive is to turn back to God! Will you listen to what the Holy Spirit is saying to you, to bring healing back to America in your own sphere of influence?

> *Don't let anyone capture you with empty philosophies and high-sounding nonsense that come from human thinking and from the spiritual powers of this world, rather than from Christ. For in Christ lives all the fullness of God in a human body. So you also are complete through your union with Christ, who is the head over every ruler and authority.* (Colossians 2:8–10)

This passage describes what happened after the fall. Humans are able to gather information and understanding from many different sources. We can get information from ourselves, other humans, Satan, and fallen angels or from Christ and the Holy Spirit. You will choose whom you will listen to.

In Christ, our union with Jesus is complete, and if you follow his leading, you will not fall, no matter what position you have in this world. Christ is over every ruler and authority, and that includes you.

10

The Temptation

Genesis 3:1–7 helps us to understand the first human temptation.

> *The serpent was the shrewdest of all the wild animals the LORD God had made. One day he asked the woman, "Did God really say you must not eat the fruit from any of the trees in the garden?"* (Genesis 3:1)

Let's look at what just occurred. The serpent is a shrewd, wild animal and had the ability to talk to Adam and Eve. Apparently, some of the animals that were created by God had the ability to communicate with our first parents. There is no indication from Adam and Eve that this communication was an unusual occurrence. They did not know that Lucifer was influencing the serpent to say the things it said. Apparently, the serpent realized he was being influenced by another power and chose to follow its leading! That is why God executed judgment on the serpent immediately after the test was complete.

> *Then the LORD God said to the serpent, "Because you have done this, you are cursed more than all animals, domestic and wild. You will crawl on your belly, groveling in the dust as long as you live."* (Genesis 3:14)

It is apparent that Lucifer had no ability to influence the mind of Adam and Eve directly; he did not get that ability until after the fall.

Since Satan is really the one asking the question, and just using the willing serpent to achieve his objective to become the ruler of this world, Lucifer is the active communicator.

Lucifer lied by altering the truth of the Word that was spoken by God to Adam. Lucifer knew what God had said to Adam:

> *"You may freely eat the fruit of every tree in the garden—except the tree of the knowledge of good and evil. If you eat its fruit, you are sure to die."*
> (Genesis 2:16–17)

Is it also possible that in this judgment, the ability of some or all animals to communicate with humans was removed?

Lucifer got them to consider that God had denied them the opportunity to partake of all the fruit. Why would God deny them the chance to know what good and evil were? Thus begins the thinking process that only spirals downward—*What else is God denying me?*

Lucifer determined that Eve was the most vulnerable in this discussion, because she received this knowledge from Adam and not from God himself. And if he could convince her, she might even become his "advocate" to Adam.

There is no information that tells us how long Adam and Eve resisted eating the forbidden fruit with the conscience that God had already given them.

> *"Of course we may eat fruit from the trees in the garden," the woman replied.* (Genesis 3:2)

Eve did not defer to Adam to communicate with the serpent, nor did Adam step in and speak the truth of what God had told him. Apparently, Adam was right there, listening to the entire conversation. I believe that Adam had no understanding of the consequences of his inaction, or the importance to establishing the truth with the serpent.

Eve continued the dialogue with Lucifer.

> *"It's only the fruit from the tree in the middle of the garden that we are not allowed to eat. God said, 'You must not eat it or even touch it; if you do, you will die.'"* (Genesis 3:3)

Eve misquoted God's Word, and Adam did not step in to correct the error. However, is it possible that Adam could have told Eve not to touch the fruit?

This illustrates how dangerous it is to add to or subtract from God's Word, or take it out of context, because it leads us down a path of a new way of thinking. This can lead to distortion and legalism.

With this uncorrected error already in Eve's mind, this gave a tremendous advantage for Lucifer in closing the deal. You see, the moment she touched the fruit and nothing happened, that would lead to an understanding in her mind that it would be okay to eat the fruit. Also, I believe that Adam and Eve, along with Lucifer, did not understand what it meant to *die,* from God's perspective.

> *"You won't die!" the serpent replied to the woman.* (Genesis 3:4)

Lucifer continued his deception.

> *"God knows that your eyes will be opened as soon as you eat it, and you will be like God, knowing both good and evil."* (Genesis 3:5)

I believe Lucifer's eyes were opened immediately, at the beginning of his action to get Adam and Eve to eat the fruit. Now Lucifer already knows both good and evil.

It appears that it was at this transition of time that all of God's creation (with free will) was going to learn what good and evil means from God's perspective and experience the consequences of their decisions.

So, what is *good?*

Everything about God is good: his love, his ways, his statutes, his laws, his judgments, and his plan. However, even today, we do not fully understand all of God's goodness, and it won't be revealed until the appropriate time. It is way beyond our understanding at this time (1 Corinthians 13:12).

So, what is *evil?*

Evil is when any of God's creation questions any part of God's love, goodness, ways, laws, and judgments or thinks their way is better than God's way. The next step of evil is when God's creation (you) rebel and refuse to obey his command. The next step in disobedience is when you convince others that it is okay not to obey the Word of God and thus alter the truth. That is when we start seeing the consequences of our rebellion. Again, evil occurs in two ways. One, when you disobey any part of God's command or law. Second, when you change the truth of God's Word and then convince another individual to disobey God's command or law (Jude 4).

How does the concept of being like God manifest itself in our lives today? Your thinking process begins to change in this dark direction when you rebel against God's authority.

You begin to reject the authority of God and his Word and then all authority.

Then you begin to believe that your way of thinking is better than God's way.

Next, you begin to justify your thinking because the Holy Spirit is trying to change your mind. You then disobey the Holy Spirit.

The next step is you get offended, and it begins to grow until it controls you.

> *And "don't sin by letting anger control you." Don't let the sun go down while you are still angry, for anger gives a foothold to the devil.* (Ephesians 4:26–27)

> *Get rid of all bitterness, rage, anger, harsh words, and slander, as well as all types of evil behavior. Instead, be kind to each other, tenderhearted, forgiving one another, just as God through Christ has forgiven you.* (Ephesians 4:31–32)

Then the offense turns into hate, and you justify your hate because of what was done to you. When your actions display bitterness, rage, and so on, you have already given Satan a foothold in your thinking.

> *Anyone who hates another brother or sister is really a murderer at heart. And you know that murderers don't have eternal life within them.* (1 John 3:15)

Please remember that this process begins in the mind.

The next step in this process is action, either in physical form or in the heart.

Then the idea of killing that person physically, or killing your relationship with the one who has offended you, begins to grow in the mind and heart.

Please understand it really does not matter what is the reason of the offense.

The next step in this process is action.

This process that occurred in the mind has fulfilled the next part of Genesis 3:5, *"knowing both good and evil."* Also, you never take into consideration what influence Satan's army played in these events. Nor do you even care.

Let's look at what will occur next in this process:

- You have determined that your way of thinking is good and right.
- You have determined that the offense is evil.
- You have passed judgment on the person or persons.
- You have determined the course of action that you will take (judgment).

Have you ever considered that these steps are God's responsibility alone, and that you have usurped God's authority? Jesus Christ himself never usurped God's authority (Philippians 2:6–11).

This occurs in every arena and area of your life; if this continues, you will refuse to allow God to rule in your life.

> *"Give us a king to judge us like all the other nations have."* . . .
>
> *"Do everything they say to you," the Lord replied, "for they are rejecting me, not you. They don't want me to be their king any longer."* (1 Samuel 8:5, 7)

These people were God's chosen people, the Jews, and they had rejected his leadership and authority. So, isn't the question today, Will I allow God to be ruler over my life, in all areas? Can you see Satan's influence on the Jews to reject the authority of God?

> *The woman [Eve] was convinced. She saw that the tree was beautiful and its fruit looked delicious, and she wanted the wisdom it would give her. So she took some of the fruit and ate it. Then she gave some to her husband, who was with her, and he ate it, too.* (Genesis 3:6)

Eve had determined in her mind that God had withheld delicious fruit and wisdom from her and saw nothing wrong with knowing good and evil.

Eve made her decision and did not ask Adam what he thought.

Adam did not offer any resistance to her decision of eating the fruit, and he willingly ate of the fruit. I believe that Adam and Eve did not fully understand the consequences of their disobedience to God's command. Nor did they understand that their disobedience proved they did not love God more than they loved the serpent.

> *"If you love me, obey my commandments."*
> (John 14:15)

Oh, how I wonder, how important is it to you to obey God's commandments?

This verse declares that if you love God, you will obey his commandments, but if you don't love him, you won't obey them!

> *Jesus replied, 'You must love the LORD your God with all your heart, all your soul, and all your mind.' This is the first and greatest commandment. A second is equally important: 'Love your neighbor as yourself.' The entire law and all the demands of the prophets are based on these two commandments."* (Matthew 22:37–40)

Do you really understand the importance of this command

in your own life and how to apply it? What is the consequence to you today if you do not obey God's commandments? Do you really understand the meaning of these verses?

Eve became Lucifer's advocate. Whose advocate will you become, Satan's or God's?

At that moment, Lucifer no longer needed the serpent to communicate to human beings.

From that time forward, Lucifer and the fallen angels have had direct access to the human mind, and many human beings have become his advocates, to get us to rebel against God, his Word, and his calling.

> *Pray, too, that we will be rescued from wicked and evil people.* (2 Thessalonians 3:2)

> *At that moment their eyes were opened, and they suddenly felt shame at their nakedness. So they sewed fig leaves together to cover themselves.* (Genesis 3:7)

The shame Adam and Eve felt because they were naked was only the beginning of the consequences of their decision. They had no idea the cost or result of their decision and how it would affect every area of their life. Let's look at what they lost or gained in their rebellion against God's command.

Adam and Eve were now spiritually separated from God.

> *Cain presented some of his crops as a gift to the Lord. Abel also brought a gift—the best portions of the firstborn lambs from his flock. The Lord accepted Abel and his gift, but he did not accept Cain and his gift.* (Genesis 4:3–5)

Once again, rebellion against God occurred, and Abel became the recipient of that rebellion. But now it comes from the DNA of Lucifer.

For women, God sharpened the pain of pregnancy. And as a result of the DNA of Lucifer, wives would desire to control their husbands, but these men would rule over them. God's judgment is a constant reminder to human beings of the consequence of rebellion against him.

For men, God cursed the ground so that men would have to struggle to scratch a living from it. Again, we see that God's judgment is a constant reminder to human beings of the consequence of rebellion against God.

God determined that humans must die in this state, until the redeemed are taken to heaven and time will be no more.

The whole earth was affected by the rebellion of Adam and Eve; everything began the process of dying.

The war began between God and Lucifer for the hearts and minds of human beings because they were given free will to choose. This war is unlike any conflict in human history.

God has determined that whoever believes in Satan's lies and serves him will receive the same judgment as all fallen angels, separated from God's kingdom and condemned to eternal punishment. All of this conflict is about who will still love God and obey his commands so they can rule and reign with him in the new kingdom.

In Matthew 7:13–14, Jesus says the following:

> *"You can enter God's Kingdom only through the narrow gate. The highway to hell is broad, and its gate is wide for the many who choose that way. But the gateway to life is very narrow and the road is difficult, and only a few ever find it."*

Do you understand that only a few will ever find the gateway to life in God's kingdom? Will you be one of the few who will enter the kingdom of God? It will be your decision who you will serve and obey.

Here is what Adam and Eve gained from their rebellion:

> *Then the Lord God said, "Look, the human beings have become like us, knowing both good and evil."*
> (Genesis 3:22)

This verse in an unintended expression of Genesis 1:26: *"Let us make human beings in our image, to be like us."* God created Adam and Eve out of love, but allowed Lucifer to tempt them with evil, and evil is to disobey God's command. Human beings would learn that obeying God's commands and laws is good, and after they have obeyed, they will be the recipients of God's blessings. God knows how he created human beings and established laws on how they should live, to make their lives full of his blessings.

Satan introduces evil into the lives of human beings, and they will learn the consequences of their disobedience to God's authority, laws, and commands.

Human beings must learn and understand how to bring their free will into obedience to God's authority, laws, and commands. Their love for God will motivate them to freely obey their Creator through the power of Jesus Christ.

Human beings must be tested and tried, and only those who are obedient as a result of saving faith will enter the kingdom of God. Going through these trials and overcoming Satan's lies will mean that disobeying God will never happen again for eternity, in the new kingdom.

Human beings, with free will, will rule and reign with Christ in obedience for eternity.

11

Lucifer's "Contribution" to God's Plan

In this chapter we will discuss the part of God's plan where he used Lucifer's rebellion to perfect the free will of angels and human beings. We must acknowledge that God knows everything, even before it happens. Everything that God does is to accomplish his ultimate will for eternity. Giving free will to angels and human beings was and remains important to God. Nothing that Lucifer did or the events that followed caught God by surprise.

> *For God's gifts and his call can never be withdrawn.*
> (Romans 11:29)

I believe this verse applies to all angels and all humanity. What did Lucifer do with his free will?

When God established that human beings would reign over all of God's created animals, Lucifer's pride overpowered his free will. He believed that God's authority should have been given to him. Lucifer became offended against God. Then he established a plan to steal and usurp that authority from human beings. Lucifer put his plan in motion and rebelled against his Creator (God). Because of his rebellion, new, dark character traits began to form and grow. Those traits include lying, hate, and unwillingness to forgive—and there is so much more.

Lucifer's pride took control, and he was unable or unwilling to forgive God for the perceived wrong. This is what happens when any of God's creation with free will don't like God's plan.

Lucifer's evil new character traits were then imparted to human beings.

Lucifer and fallen angels hate God, and they have no self-control over it. The power over lies and hate and the ability to forgive only come from God, and Lucifer and his angels have chosen their destiny. I have heard so many times from people who declare that they hate God because he allowed something to happen that they did not understand. Will you be one of those who will believe Satan's lie?

Human beings are created in the image of God (Genesis 1:27); therefore, Lucifer had an absolute hatred for God's new creation (those human beings).

Lucifer and the fallen angels are united in their goal, namely, to destroy human beings, and to use anything or anyone to keep human beings from being reconciled with God and enjoying a restored relationship with him. Lucifer's objective of hate extends to keeping human beings from loving one another.

Satan and all his forces, angelic and human servants, accomplish this task by feeding you lies so that you will deny the truth of God's Word. They get people to change the meaning of God's Word so that it will be more acceptable to your heart and mind so that you will believe Satan's lies.

> *Stay alert! Watch out for your great enemy, the devil. He prowls around like a roaring lion, looking for someone to devour.* (1 Peter 5:8)

Lucifer has no desire, knowledge, or ability to help you grow closer to God! His only objective is to destroy you and separate you from the love of God. Will you separate yourself from the love of God and give up?

> *You used to live in sin, just like the rest of the world, obeying the devil—the commander of the powers in the unseen world. He is the spirit at work in the hearts of those who refuse to obey God.* (Ephesians 2:2)

How can you deny the truth of God's Word? The spirit of Satan is at work in the hearts of those who refuse to obey God's laws. You can recognize them by their actions.

Lucifer will be allowed to rule the world for seven years, known as the tribulation. This will be accomplished through the Antichrist, and he will claim to be God during the last three and a-half years of the same seven years.

Lucifer and the fallen angels already know they are defeated and know their destiny (Matthew 8:28–29). Lucifer has been effective in disguising his influence on humans, even to the point that today, humanity rejects the idea that humans can be controlled by the powers of darkness. All you have to do is look at all the killing and rebellion against all authority that are going on in our society today. Are we going to deny the truth of the evidence that we see every day? In the end, what are you going to do with your free will?

Since God knew what was in Lucifer's heart, the Lord established a plan to use Satan's rebellion to perfect his creation—human beings and angels. The trials and tribulations that you will go through will help you grow stronger in God's power and prepare you to be faithful to God for eternity. Through these same trials and tribulations, you discover how dependent you are on God's power, to bring your free will in obedience to God's will. The question I have is, Will you allow God to perfect you for his kingdom (1 Corinthians 1:25)?

God has given you a choice to make, and you are going to decide where you will spend eternity.

SECTION 3

The Plan for Human Beings

12

God's Divine Plan: Your Call to Participate in Building the Kingdom of God

Let's examine Genesis 1:26–27 and discover what it means to be created in the image of God.

> *Then God said, "Let us make human beings in our image, to be like us. They will reign over the fish in the sea, the birds in the sky, the livestock, all the wild animals on the earth, and the small animals that scurry along the ground." So God created human beings in his own image. In the image of God he created them; male and female he created them.*

Human beings are the only creation ever created in the image of God. So how are you different from angels?

Let's list some of the characteristics/attributes of God:

- Love
- Creator
- Mercy
- Wisdom
- Omniscience (all-knowing)
- Judgment
- Forgiveness
- Grace

- Patience
- Long-suffering
- Kindness
- Power
- Generosity
- Teacher
- Guide
- Joy
- Hope
- Justice
- Healer
- Authority

This new human race was created with a brain with the capacity to grow, learn, and understand the natural laws that reveal to you how great God is.

God made human beings to be co-creators with him. I believe this occurs in two ways.

When you procreate and have children, you begin to learn what it is like to love like God—to nurture, train, guide, and discipline your children just like God does with you. Yet, you know there will be a day when your children will make their own decisions, because their free will takes over. All the while, you want so much for your children to make good decisions. You learn what it is like when they don't make the right decisions—all the pain, sorrow, and anguish you feel for them—just like God does for you when you make unhealthy decisions. The other side of free will is when you teach your children and they are obedient, and even exceed your expectations, what joy and hope you have for them! This experience happens with all family members. In contrast, angels (who are not made in the image of God) have no knowledge, understanding, or comprehension of these divine attributes.

Before human beings are born, they are given talents and abilities by God to become co-creators in this world today. We are able to create things out of the resources that God has already made available. Before human beings were created, everything that was made was created by God. Now, angels can only watch in amazement at what God has done through human beings. You should never lose sight of everything you are, and everything that you are able to do has been given to you by God!

Yet, Satan has been effective in convincing us that all was accomplished by our own power and ability, and so we don't give God the credit. Can we see what pride has done to our society?

When the Word of God says, *"In the image of God he created them; male and female he created them,"* what does this mean? I believe he created Adam and Eve to be in perfect harmony with each other, having no strife, no division, and only to complement each other. They lived in perfect unity, just like the Trinity, in how they functioned as one and yet had different responsibilities to achieve the same goal.

We can see the consequences of their disobedience in Genesis 3:16: *"Then he said to the woman . . . 'You will desire to control your husband, but he will rule over you.'"* So now, infused with Satan's DNA, we have lost the total unity to achieve the same goal between a husband and his wife.

Not only did God call angels to care for people who will inherit salvation; God has also called you to be a witness to other human beings who will inherit salvation.

Here are some questions for you to consider:

- Will you love God's creation like he does?
- Do you understand the judgment that awaits those who won't accept Jesus Christ?
- Do you understand the bondage or captivity that all humanity has been held in since Adam and Eve?
- Do you recognize and see the consequences in our world today, the rebellion against God's authority and the authority God has delegated to others?
- Do you recognize that every human being needs a Savior, a redeemer, because we were born sinners with the infused DNA of Satan?
- Are you willing to forgive and love your fellow man so you can be a witness of the love of Jesus Christ that you now have?
- Do you understand the battle that is raging because God loves you and Satan hates you, along with all of humanity?
- Do you realize your actions reveal who rules your life?
- Do you realize that by studying God's Word you will receive the power needed to enable you to live a holy

life—if you commit the truth of God's Word to your heart and mind?
- Since you have free will, do you understand why you will be tested and tried in this life?

> *"But you will receive power when the Holy Spirit comes upon you. And you will be my witnesses, telling people about me everywhere—in Jerusalem, throughout Judea, in Samaria, and to the ends of the earth."* (Acts 1:8)

So many professing Christians today deny the power of the Holy Spirit working in their life in order to witness to people about Jesus Christ. Satan has been successful in convincing many in our generation that the Holy Spirit's role and purpose are not for us today. The problem is we begin to reject and deny the voice of the Holy Spirit in our hearts and minds. Then we begin to think we can do things by our own power, and so, in our minds, we don't need the Holy Spirit.

What arrogance and pride have engulfed our thinking! You will receive power from the Holy Spirit to accomplish what you are called to do, and that is to be a witness and tell people about Jesus Christ. So, what are you going to do? Will you listen to the leading of the Holy Spirit so that you will witness to others about Jesus, or will you reject the gentle leading of the Holy Spirit?

> *God himself has prepared us for this, and as a guarantee he has given us his Holy Spirit. . . . And all of this is a gift from God, who brought us back to himself through Christ. And God has given us this task of reconciling people to him.* (2 Corinthians 5:5, 18)

God has prepared you from the time you committed your life to Jesus and allowed his love to control you to receive the Holy Spirit. The Holy Spirit was given to you to make sure you have the power to accomplish all that you are called to do. The Holy Spirit's work will continue even up to the point of receiving your new glorified body, as long as you don't turn your back on God's love for you. You will choose your destiny, where you will spend eternity.

Everything that God gives you is a free gift. However, it also comes with the responsibility to have a sincere heart and no longer live for yourself (because you have died to your old life). One of the most difficult tasks to achieve is to stop evaluating others from a human point of view. We need to seek the wisdom of the Holy Spirit on how to reconcile people to Jesus, because we can't do it on our own.

> *God has given each of you a gift from his great variety of spiritual gifts. Use them well to serve one another.* (1 Peter 4:10)

This verse establishes that every redeemed believer has been given at least one gift that will help you to serve one another.

> *Those who belong to Christ Jesus have nailed the passions and desires of their sinful nature to his cross and crucified them there. Since we are living by the Spirit, let us follow the Spirit's leading in every part of our lives. Let us not become conceited, or provoke one another, or be jealous of one another.* (Galatians 5:24–26)

You know you will choose whether or not you will believe the plain and simple truth of the Word of God. It is important to not be deceived, and so you must examine yourself. This passage begins by making a statement about those who belong to Christ Jesus, namely, that they have nailed the passions and desires of their sinful natures to the cross of Christ Jesus.

If you are a believer, this is done spiritually by the power of the Holy Spirit that has been given to you. The Holy Spirit will teach you everything you need to know on how to live for Christ in every area of your life. Your love for Jesus is what motivates you to change your actions, because your goal is to become like Jesus—to love, forgive, and obey God just like Jesus Christ did. Now you have the power to live that kind of life! Remember, Satan's influence is going to tell you that you don't have the power to stop sinning. Why? Because Satan is a liar!

> *Those who have been born into God's family do not make a practice of sinning, because God's life is in them. So they can't keep on sinning, because they are children of God. So now we can tell who are children of God and who are children of the devil. Anyone who does not live*

> *righteously and does not love other believers does not belong to God.* (1 John 3:9–10)

A question is, What does it mean if you are born again and stop making a practice of sinning?

Also, what does it mean that *"God's life is in them"* (those who have *"been born into God's family"*)?

These verses describe the inner action within a born-again Christian by the Holy Spirit (which is what is meant by *"God's life"*). Satan's DNA is infused into the genetics of every human being, and this never goes away as long as you live in your earthly body. However, when you are born again, the Holy Spirit, who now lives inside you, reveals to you the Word of God and what sin is. This spiritual warfare for your mind and heart never stops as long as you are alive. So now it is up to you. Whom will you believe and serve? If you obey the Holy Spirit, you will start to become an overcomer to the power of Satan's DNA through the power of God's Spirit. Your actions, what you say, and the way you live are the evidence of who controls you. You must recognize the results of your own decisions and not be deceived. If you follow the leading of the Holy Spirit, you will sin less and less, and your love for Jesus will grow stronger day by day.

This passage continues to state that you will be able to distinguish between the children of God and the children of the devil. It also establishes that if you don't follow the leading of the Holy Spirit, you can't live righteously, and you will not be able to love other believers. If this is happening, then you do not belong to God.

> *Then the Lord said, "I have seen how stubborn and rebellious these people are. Now leave me alone so my fierce anger can blaze against them, and I will destroy them. Then I will make you, Moses, into a great nation."*
>
> *But Moses tried to pacify the Lord his God. . . . "Turn away from your fierce anger. Change your mind about this terrible disaster you have threatened against your people!"* (Exodus 32:9–12)

These verses represent an amazing discussion between God and Moses.

The influence and the power that Satan had over God's chosen people had become evident. Despite the miraculous deliverance from Egypt that they all witnessed by the power of the unseen God, they still rebelled. Through the plagues, every god that the Egyptians worshipped and believed in was proven by God to have no power over him. God's chosen people became firsthand witnesses to the total destruction of every Egyptian god their oppressors had served.

In Egypt, Satan had convinced the Jews and established in the hearts and minds that they needed a God that they could see. So, Aaron made a golden calf and altar so the people could worship and declare that this idol was the god who had delivered them from Egypt. They actually reduced God to an idol in their hearts and minds.

This event again reinforces the idea that God knows the hearts and the minds of his chosen people and knows the rebellion that Satan has inspired in them. God gave the Ten Commandments to Moses to give to his chosen people. These commandments were going to establish laws that would address and correct the lies of Satan. These laws would establish in writing how to worship God and how to live with others. The conscience that God gave mankind had been overpowered by Satan's lies. That is why they were written on stone tablets so they would never be forgotten.

God made this statement to Moses: "*Now leave me alone so my fierce anger [judgment] can blaze against them, and I will destroy them [all].*" And then he offered Moses an alternative to his covenant to make him into a great nation (Exodus 32:10).

God was now establishing for Moses that he (God) is holy, and his judgment must occur now for the disobedience of these stubborn people. Yet God already knew that Moses was going to plead for them, and he did. I believe that God wanted Moses to also love his people enough to petition him to postpone his holy judgment to fulfill his earlier oath that he had made to Abraham, Isaac, and Jacob.

God allowed Moses to execute judgment on these rebellious people, and so three thousand were killed—people who plainly declared they were not on the Lord's side.

Today you must consider another way that you can influence God on behalf of your enemies in a way that could increase the number of people who give their hearts to God.

Since God has given us love for human beings, we are active advocates to petition God to postpone judgment on people in order to give them more time to turn to Jesus Christ. You know Satan is your accuser before God; now are you going to accuse your enemies just like Satan before God? How do we demonstrate to God our love for human beings today and become an advocate for them? Consider Jesus's request to God the Father and Stephen's request to the Lord.

> *Jesus said, "Father, forgive them, for they don't know what they are doing."* (Luke 23:34)

It seems to me that no one involved in this situation understood God's redemptive plan. I would even declare that none of them realized Lucifer's direct influence and deception on their thinking process or motives. I believe that Jesus Christ was asking God to forgive them, to give them more time, so more revelation could be revealed and knowledge could be understood so they could have an opportunity to accept Jesus Christ. Otherwise, immediate judgment from God would be required.

> *As they stoned him, Stephen prayed, "Lord Jesus, receive my spirit." He fell to his knees, shouting, "Lord, don't charge them with this sin!" And with that, he died.* (Acts 7:59–60)

Consider Saul's/Paul's involvement in Stephen's death. I believe that Stephen's request of the Lord to not charge his executioners with this sin gives us an insight into Stephen's heart. Stephen understood God's ultimate consequences for murder. So, Stephen petitioned the Lord not to hold this sin against his killers, which would give these murderers more time to come to know Jesus Christ as their personal Savior. This would have included Saul/Paul—in addition to others whom we don't know about, so that God would postpone his judgment on these individuals. You see, it is appointed unto man once to die, and then follows the judgment. Stephen understood the importance of trying to reach the lost, even through his death. We see Stephen following the example that Jesus set to petition God not to charge them with the sin of killing an innocent man. Why? Because they didn't understand the influence that Satan had on their actions. They were spiritually blind and could not see how deeply that influence had penetrated their hearts. In your day of trouble, will you have the love and power of Jesus Christ to petition God not to charge the sins committed against you by your accusers?

> *They rushed at him [Stephen] and dragged him out of the city and began to stone him. His accusers took off their coats and laid them at the feet of a young man named Saul.* (Acts 7:57–58)

Because Saul was spiritually blind, this Pharisee of Pharisees was a great advocate for Satan. Saul was a great example of someone who was deceived by Satan. In his heart and mind, he believed he was doing God's will in killing Christians. (We don't know how many Christians he had executed in his position of authority.) Saul became Paul sometime after the divine revelation that he was not, in fact, doing anything close to God's revealed will. Jesus illustrated the truth to Saul through his blindness, and then sent Ananias to restore Saul's sight. Saul was now able to see both physically and spiritually. Paul became a great servant of the kingdom of God.

> *Don't just pretend to love others. Really love them. Hate what is wrong. Hold tightly to what is good. Love each other with genuine affection.* (Romans 12:9–10)

I believe that when Paul said, *"Hold tightly to what is good,"* he was indicating that your adversaries, the devil's advocates, will try to convince you not to follow through with God's way of overcoming evil. You can hate the evil that someone does, but not the person, because you understand the war of the flesh and the depth of Satan's influence on that individual. Just love and pray for others and give the Holy Spirit time to convince that person to obey God's Word.

> *Instead, "If your enemies are hungry, feed them. If they are thirsty, give them something to drink. In doing this, you will heap burning coals of shame on their heads."*

> *Don't let evil conquer you, but conquer evil by doing good.* (Romans 12:20–21)

I believe the key to these verses is to understand what evil means. Who or what is evil? Evil is Satan and his influence in trying to get you to disobey God and get you to think like he (Satan) does, and then to act accordingly. Satan can conquer you if you don't follow the lead of the Holy Spirit and demonstrate love to your enemies. But you have the power to conquer evil because your love for Jesus has changed the way you think and how you interact with others, even those who are hostile to the gospel. You see, your enemies don't understand this way of thinking.

The question is, Are you going to become an active participant in winning the lost? Are you going to willingly be an advocate for Jesus Christ and do it his way, or do it your way? Again, you will choose how you represent Jesus Christ to the human beings that you come in contact with every day. You must always recognize that Lucifer's influence in the form of evil is trying to get you to refuse to do it God's way.

> *A final word: Be strong in the Lord and in his mighty power.* (Ephesians 6:10)

This verse establishes a truth that you can be strong in the Lord because of his mighty power in you. Yet, how many times do you say to yourself, "I can't overcome that sin"? Don't you understand that is a lie from Satan? Have you become spiritually blind again? It is so important that you understand the war between good (God) and evil (Satan).

> *Put on all of God's armor so that you will be able to stand firm against all strategies of the devil.* (Ephesians 6:11)

This verse establishes an important command that you must put on all of God's armor. You may ask, "Why, if I am already a Christian?" So that you will be able to accomplish your calling (to win the lost) and be like Jesus Christ. It also states that you will not be able to stand firm if you don't put on the armor of God. Now you must understand what it means to stand against all the strategies of the devil. Satan and his advocates will strategize ways to attack you so that you will give up and then reject Jesus Christ and lose your love for him. If Satan's advocates are not successful in destroying your love for God, then their objective will be to reduce your influence on the lost. This does not have to happen, because you have been given the power of Jesus and the armor has been made available to you—if you are willing to put it on. I believe your love for Jesus Christ is what will motivate you to put on the whole armor of God and hate sin!

> *For we are not fighting against flesh-and-blood enemies, but against evil rulers and authorities of the unseen world, against mighty powers in this dark world, and against evil spirits in the heavenly places.*
> (Ephesians 6:12)

This verse establishes who the real enemies are, namely, Satan, evil rulers, authorities of the unseen world, mighty powers in the dark world, and evil spirits in heavenly places. Not human beings.

In our society today, Satan has blinded us to this truth. We no longer recognize the deception in our hearts and minds. We refuse to acknowledge the influence that Satan's forces have on individual human beings. So, we then reject the power of God and his Word, which is the only means by which our land and society can be healed from the evil forces that have overtaken us. Can you see the results of our spiritual blindness in our world today?

> *Therefore, put on every piece of God's armor so you will be able to resist the enemy in the time of evil. Then after the battle you will still be standing firm.* (Ephesians 6:13)

Now that you understand who your enemy is, does that create in you a greater desire to put on the whole armor of God? You are the one who determines how much of the armor you put on. Please never forget your enemy is going to make every effort to sidetrack you, like getting you too busy with the things of this world. This verse also establishes that your enemies will select how they will confront you within the parameters of almighty God. I believe you can lose sight of the reality that you going through a battle. These types of distractions can be devastating to your spiritual walk. However, this verse declares that if you put on the whole armor of God, you will be victorious and not lose your faith in Jesus Christ.

> *Stand your ground, putting on the belt of truth and the body armor of God's righteousness.* (Ephesians 6:14)

You must stand your ground. That means the battle will be hard, but everything about the Godhead is truthful, including the Word of God. The Holy Spirit who lives in you will give you truth, and then truth will flow out of you—if you obey. Truth holds the body armor together. Satan's forces will continue to lie about every aspect of God's truth, trying to undermine your foundation in Jesus Christ. If Satan's forces can get you to believe in just one lie, he can establish a stronghold in your life. So, guard the truth of God in your heart and mind, and understand the war or battle continues even today.

You need to understand that your obedience to the leading of the Holy Spirit produces righteousness, and that comes from God. Your character absolutely changes when you put on the armor of God. Everything about you changes: the way you think, the things you say, the places you go. You begin to examine everything in light of God's Word, through the leading of the Holy Spirit.

> *For shoes, put on the peace that comes from the Good News so that you will be fully prepared.*
> (Ephesians 6:15)

Your new life is a journey, and you need peace in knowing that you are going in the right direction because your enemy (Satan) is going to lie to you. It is so important for you to study the Word of God so the Holy Spirit can give you peace. As you study the Word of God, the Holy Spirit reveals to you the truth and gives you understanding on how to apply it to your life in every situation. All you need to do is obey. You will never be prepared if you don't know the Word of God. You will be easily deceived if you don't know the truth of God's Word.

> *In addition to all of these, hold up the shield of faith to stop the fiery arrows of the devil.* (Ephesians 6:16)

What is the foundation of your faith? When you gave your heart, mind, and life to Jesus Christ, you basically said, "I know your way is the only way to live," and you love everything about him. That was the beginning of your faith. Now your faith must grow stronger through the reading of God's Word. You must allow the Holy Spirit to reveal the truth of God's Word in your spirit, which will give you understanding. That knowledge will be necessary in your daily combat with Satan's forces.

The study of God's Word benefits you and those whom you witness to because you are able to speak truth to them. This verse continues to declare that the devil and his forces are not going to stop their attack on you. Their objective is to destroy your faith in Jesus Christ, God's Word, and the Holy Spirit. What will you decide? Will you put on the whole armor of God, or will you decide you don't need it? The consequences of your decision are eternal!

> *Put on salvation as your helmet, and take the sword of the Spirit, which is the word of God.* (Ephesians 6:17)

Your belief in Jesus Christ is the basis of your salvation. That knowledge is the helmet that protects your mind from Satan's lies. This verse continues by declaring that you must take the sword of the Spirit, which is the Word of God. This is a spiritual battle. The Holy Spirit teaches you how to use the Word of God, which is sharper than any two-edged sword. The Holy Spirit gives you knowledge and understanding of how to witness to the lost and counter the lies of Satan's forces.

> *Pray in the Spirit at all times and on every occasion. Stay alert and be persistent in your prayers for all believers everywhere.* (Ephesians 6:18)

This passage establishes the importance of communicating with (and praying in) the Holy Spirit. How often should you do this? This should become a way of life, so you must recognize that you need to be led by the Holy Spirit to accomplish what you are called to do by God. You need to recognize this truth in your heart and mind because the power in you (the Holy Spirit) is greater than the power in the world (Satan's forces). The reason that you pray for all believers everywhere is that you understand they are in the same battle as you.

The full armor of God has been made available to you, but you must put it on because you love God and you want to accomplish what God has called you to do and you hate sin in your life.

Can you, a disciple of Jesus Christ, be influenced by Satan? This scriptural illustration gives you spiritual understanding of why you must put on the armor of God.

> *Then he [Jesus] asked them, "But who do you say I am?"*
>
> *Simon Peter answered, "You are the Messiah, the Son of the living God."*
>
> *Jesus replied, "You are blessed, Simon son of John, because my Father in heaven has revealed this to you. You did not learn this from any human being."* (Matthew 16:15–17)

Peter, a disciple of Jesus Christ, answered a question given to the disciples by Jesus. Jesus revealed to Peter and the disciples how Peter had received this knowledge. Peter didn't realize how he had received this truth, and he may have even wondered where it came from. Jesus described how divine revelation occurs. Jesus told Peter that he was blessed because God had chosen him (Peter) to reveal who Jesus was. God determined that it was now time to reveal this truth to the disciples.

> *From then on Jesus began to tell his disciples plainly that it was necessary for him to go to Jerusalem, and that he would suffer many terrible things at the hands of the elders, the leading priests, and the teachers of religious law. He would be killed, but on the third day he would be raised from the dead.* (Matthew 16:21)

Jesus was giving the disciples more divine revelation of events that must take place, and in this case, even to the day and time that prophecy would be fulfilled. But the disciples did not comprehend the plan of God. But just a few minutes later, Peter made another statement to Jesus after Jesus told them about what was going to happen.

> *But Peter took him [Jesus] aside and began to reprimand him for saying such things. "Heaven forbid, Lord," he said. "This will never happen to you!"*
>
> *Jesus turned to Peter and said, "Get away from me, Satan! You are a dangerous trap to me. You are seeing things merely from a human point of view, not from God's."* (Matthew 16:22–23)

Peter had just become Satan's advocate after Satan introduced a thought into his mind. Peter reasoned in his mind that if he called on heaven to forbid these events to occur, they would be stopped. It doesn't matter that Satan's motive was different from Peter's. Jesus rebuked Satan because Jesus knew where this thought was coming from (Satan), and then acknowledged that he (Jesus) had already been confronted with this temptation from Satan.

This was already a battle in Jesus's mind, and it was not resolved until Jesus prayed in the Garden of Gethsemane, asking, *"My Father! If it is possible, let this cup of suffering be taken away from me. Yet I want your will to be done, not mine"* (Matthew 26:39). Peter just didn't know he was being influenced by Satan.

These passages reveal that Peter, a disciple of Jesus Christ, was influenced to speak from two different sources—and he didn't realize the truth of what had just occurred. It wasn't until Jesus gave divine revelation to Peter and the disciples that they began to understand that there are two spiritual sources of influence that could influence their actions. That is why it is so important to put on the whole armor of God, so you will have a spiritual understanding of why you think the way you do. You have free will to choose whom you will believe and obey.

Who is influencing the person who kills another human being, the person who lies, the person who is unable to forgive, the person who hates another, or the person who commits adultery? Because of the influence of Satan's forces, these actions are committed by individuals who may not recognize the source of the temptation. I only named a few of the sins in the spectrum of possibilities that a person can be tempted to do.

Who is influencing the person who tells the truth, the person who is able to forgive, the person who is able to love his or her enemy, the person who is able to be faithful to their spouse, and so on? It is obedience to the truth of God's Word.

To summarize: How do you put on the whole armor of God? It is by studying the Word of God and recognizing that it is the truth and then committing that truth to your heart and mind so you will be able to obey the Word of God. Then your love, faith, and belief in God will grow stronger day by day. The Holy Spirit will reveal the power of your salvation, and then you will able to witness to others because you know what the Word of God says. The Holy Spirit will guide you in all your ways if you will listen and obey.

What will Satan's forces do in response? Their objective will be to get you to believe Satan's lies, to deny the truth of the Word of God, and to believe that it is okay to disobey God, Jesus Christ, and the Holy Spirit. Satan's forces will do all they can to try to destroy your love for God, your faith, and your belief in God. Your actions will reveal who you have chosen to believe.

Can you defend yourself from the thoughts from Satan's forces, whether they are from evil spirits or human beings?

> *We are human, but we don't wage war as humans do.*
> (2 Corinthians 10:3)

Never forget, you are in a continuous war every day, but you are restricted on how you wage this war. Satan and his fallen angels can only influence your thought process. Because they are not omniscient (all-knowing), they cannot read your mind. If you give in to Satan's influence, you will react differently than if you were obedient to God's Word. Never forget this spiritual war is real—you are fighting for your life, whether you like it or not.

> *We use God's mighty weapons, not worldly weapons, to knock down the strongholds of human reasoning and to*

> *destroy false arguments.* (2 Corinthians 10:4)

What are God's mighty weapons that he has given to you? You have the power of the Word of God, the power of the Holy Spirit in you, the power to forgive, the power to love your enemies, the power to tell the truth, the power to be faithful to your spouse, and so on, all because you love Jesus Christ (the Word) and you believe and have put your faith and trust in him.

Watch out! As Satan's forces try to influence you, your human reasoning will be activated and you will try to justify sinning against God's Word. This all begins in the mind and the thought process that leads to (fallen) human reasoning. Don't take the bait; resist the influence of Satan's forces because you have the power to resist and overcome their lies—if you believe the Word of God. Don't deny the power that you have been given.

> *We destroy every proud obstacle that keeps people from knowing God. We capture their rebellious thoughts and teach them to obey Christ.* (2 Corinthians 10:5)

You destroy every proud obstacle that keeps you from knowing God, and you accomplish this through obeying the Word of God. Your pride will destroy your relationship with Jesus Christ, because your reasoning believes you can do it your way and not God's way. The rebellious thoughts originate from Satan's forces; however, your obedience to the Word of God and the Holy Spirit strengthens your relationship with Jesus Christ day by day.

13

How Will You Represent Jesus Christ?

Because of God's grace to me, I have laid the foundation like an expert builder. Now others are building on it. But whoever is building on this foundation must be very careful. For no one can lay any foundation other than the one we already have—Jesus Christ.

—1 Corinthians 3:10–11

Paul recognized that God gave him grace. Grace encompasses mercy, forgiveness, power, gifts, God's call, and God's love. Paul understood that he was charged with presenting and representing Jesus Christ as the foundation of winning the lost. Paul also recognized the importance of following the leading of the Lord and doing it the Lord's way—hence being an expert builder of the kingdom of God.

Paul also recognized that he was not the only one who was going to build the kingdom of God. If you are born again, you are a builder who is also a part of a team. Do you follow the leading of the Lord in everything you do and say? Always remember that it is not about you or what you think should be done or even how to do it. The Lord's way is the only right way.

In today's professing religious culture, there is a common saying: "There are many ways to get to heaven." In other words, there are many different religions, and they all lead to salvation.

Again I declare, there is only one way to heaven, and that is through Jesus Christ—and none other. If you refuse to believe the truth, that Jesus Christ is the only way to heaven, then you are doing the same thing that Lucifer did in the Garden of Eden. You are misrepresenting the truth of God's Word. Will you receive the same judgment as Satan? It is so important that you speak the truth of God's Word and not Satan's lies.

> *Anyone who builds on that foundation may use a variety of materials—gold, silver, jewels, wood, hay, or straw.* (1 Corinthians 3:12)

In our endeavor to be a witness of Jesus Christ (who is the foundation of our faith), this verse describes different building materials. Jesus allows us the freedom to choose how we win the lost. How will you build the kingdom of God, his way or your way?

Gold, silver, and jewels are your works that are the product of love and following the leading of the Holy Spirit (and then doing it God's way). Your testimony/witness should be motivated by the love of Jesus Christ and the love of others.

Wood, hay, and straw are your works that represent actions done without love and doing it your way. You can get to the place where you do things out of habit, and you forget that everything you do and say are representing Jesus Christ. This can occur in your everyday living.

Do you forget to ask your Lord daily for the love and wisdom needed to deal with your troubles and trials that are going to come your way? Your adversaries are on a mission to keep you from doing God's will in your life. This is all about how you are building the kingdom of God.

> *But on the judgment day, fire will reveal what kind of work each builder has done. The fire will show if a person's work has any value.* (1 Corinthians 3:13)

Your judgment day is coming, and God will examine your motives, your actions, your thinking, your obedience. All will be revealed to you, and nothing will be hidden from anyone in attendance. This examination will reveal the quality of your works, and God will determine if they had any value in building the kingdom of God. When this time or event occurs, it will be too late for you to change anything. On this day, God is establishing with you the importance of obedience to him in a way that you never comprehended before.

The fire of this sacred evaluation represents God's holiness, and your work will be examined, judged, and revealed for everyone to see. What you thought was hidden will be exposed. It is sad that so many of your teachers may have told you that discipleship has nothing to do with works. The fact of the matter is, if you are redeemed in Christ Jesus (saved), everything you do and say is a testimony of who you serve—and all of it equals works. You are either building the kingdom of God or undermining that kingdom. The decision is yours! Do you want Jesus to say to you, "*Well done, my good and faithful servant*"? (Matthew 25:21).

These verses describe how God will examine you!

What is your responsibility and the consequence if you don't follow the leading of the Holy Spirit? Because your calling (work) is to build the kingdom of God in cooperation with Jesus Christ and the Holy Spirit.

> "*Whenever you receive a message from me, warn people immediately.*" (Ezekiel 3:17)

When the Holy Spirit gives you a spiritual unction to witness to a person, your responsibility is to respond immediately because the circumstances and time are right. Are you always listening to what the Holy Spirit is saying to you?

> "*If I warn the wicked, saying, 'You are under the penalty of death,' but you fail to deliver the warning, they will die in their sins. And I will hold you responsible for their deaths.*" (Ezekiel 3:18)

It is important to give the warning that the Holy Spirit gives you, because it is a matter of life and death and the consequences extend out into eternity. What is the consequence if you fail to deliver the warning? You have denied someone the opportunity to be forgiven of their sins and to be set free from Satan's power to become a servant of Jesus Christ. And you will be held responsible for their spiritual death without God. I believe if you are not obedient to warn that person or you don't do it immediately, then your disobedience is like wood, hay, or straw, and you will lose your reward. You might even say that's okay. Really, you're okay with that person going to hell for eternity when your influence might have helped that person to accept Jesus Christ as their Savior? Do you want to be a vessel led by the Holy Spirit to win the lost? Then you must obey! Your work of wood, hay, or straw will never survive the fire of God's holiness, and it will be burned up for all to see!

> *"If you warn them and they refuse to repent and keep on sinning, they will die in their sins. But you will have saved yourself because you obeyed me."*
> (Ezekiel 3:19)

If you obey the Holy Spirit and the person refuses to repent and continues to sin, then they will die in their sins and be separated from God and live in hell for eternity. I believe when you obey the Holy Spirit, your work is like gold, silver, or jewels, and your work will be rewarded because of your obedience, and you have saved yourself from the loss of your reward.

> *"If righteous people turn away from their righteous behavior and ignore the obstacles I put in their way, they will die. And if you do not warn them, they will die in their sins. None of their righteous acts will be remembered, and I will hold you responsible for their deaths."*
> (Ezekiel 3:20)

This describes a person who is born again who turns from their righteous behavior and starts sinning again without repentance. A person's righteous behavior is only achieved through the power of Jesus Christ, and that power enables them to stop sinning. It also describes God's active response to their disobedience by putting obstacles in their life trying to get that person to repent so their sins can be forgiven.

The Holy Spirit can choose you to be one of the obstacles to help motivate them to stop sinning and repent. However, I believe if that person refuses to stop sinning, then none of their righteous acts will be remembered, including (that which we call) their salvation. I will interject a New Testament verse that also describes this judgment, and you can decide for yourself.

> *"On judgment day many will say to me, 'Lord! Lord! We prophesied in your name and cast out demons in your name and performed many miracles in your name.'"* (Matthew 7:22)

These individuals, who are many, are at their judgment, and it is too late to change their verdict. These individuals state a truth to Jesus Christ about the works they did for him, and they are surprised or shocked at the evaluation. You must understand that they couldn't do these works in Jesus's name without being a servant. I believe this illustrates what happens to a righteous person who goes back to sinning without repentance.

> *"But I will reply, 'I never knew you. Get away from me, you who break God's laws.'"* (Matthew 7:23)

This describes what happens when a person who is righteous and does works in the power of Jesus Christ goes back to sinning or breaking God's law. None of their righteous deeds or their salvation will be remembered. I believe in our society today we look at sin differently than God does. Is it time to examine yourself to determine if you are in the faith?

Let's go back to the analysis of Ezekiel 3:20.

If someone dies in their sins, that means their current sins are not forgiven and they die separated from God and will live in hell for eternity. You might say, "How could that happen?"

Because that person chose to deny the power of Jesus Christ that would have given them the power to stop sinning and make them holy (2 Timothy 3:5).

That verse also states that if you refuse to warn them, the consequence of your disobedience is that they will die in their sins because this could be their last opportunity to repent.

When the Holy Spirit commissions you to warn a person, do it his way and not your way. If you refuse to obey, the consequence to you is that the work you were given to do will become like wood, hay, or straw, and it will not survive the fire of God's holiness. You will suffer the loss of your reward, and all will see that God judges righteously.

> *"But if you warn righteous people not to sin and they listen to you and do not sin, they will live, and you will have saved yourself, too."* (Ezekiel 3:21)

This describes a person who is born again who stops sinning due to your warning and they will live and not die (spiritually) in their sins because they repented.

Because you were obedient and followed the leading of the Holy Spirit, a person was forgiven and your work was like gold, silver, or jewels, and you will receive a reward, and all will see that God judges righteously.

Let's go back to the analysis of 1 Corinthians 3:14:

> *If the work survives, that builder will receive a reward.* (1 Corinthians 3:14)

The works that survive the fiery examination will be rewarded. God determines my reward and the responsibility I will have in the new kingdom! Please remember, all this occurs from God's point of view, not mine.

I have heard a countless number of professing Christians claim that God's reward, which he wants to give them, is not that important!

Why?

Do I need to examine my motives? Why do I serve God? Do I love God to the point that I want to do his will? Do I love others enough that I want them to go to heaven? God has established this plan and has determined that it is his desire to reward his children who are victorious over Satan and his advocates (through the power of Jesus Christ). Who am I to reject a reward that God wants to give me out of his love? Where is that coming from? Is your pride taking over?

> *But if the work is burned up, the builder will suffer great loss. The builder will be saved, but like someone barely escaping through a wall of flames.*
> (1 Corinthians 3:15)

However, if my work does not survive the fiery examination, I will suffer great loss. When it says I will suffer great loss, this is from God's perspective, and I really don't have any idea what God has prepared for me. Apparently, I will be able to see, hear, and understand my loss, along with everyone else in attendance.

On this earth, I have suffered loss, but does it even compare to what I could lose at my judgment?

> *No eye has seen, no ear has heard, and no mind has imagined what God has prepared for those who love him.* (1 Corinthians 2:9)

According to 1 Corinthians 3:10–15, everyone involved in this judgment is saved. However, the rest of verse 15 gives us a picture of someone barely escaping through a wall of flames.

Oh, how we take for granted God's love and mercy, Jesus Christ's death and shedding his blood for us, and the Holy Spirit living in us and teaching us God's ways!

> *Don't you realize that all of you together are the temple of God and that the Spirit of God lives in you?*
> (1 Corinthians 3:16)

All born-again human beings are making choices and decisions on how they are going to live every day. All of us together are the temple of God (where the Spirit of God lives—in us), and our choices and decisions matter. We are either glorifying God in our obedience every day or defiling the temple where the Spirit of God lives. If we are defiling the temple of God, we must repent and stop sinning.

We must never forget that we have been given power over sin, so we don't have to sin anymore.

> *God will destroy anyone who destroys this temple. For God's temple is holy, and you are that temple.*
> (1 Corinthians 3:17)

The consequence of a believer who refuses to repent and turn back to God is that they will be destroyed in hell, separated from God. This person, who was a believer, will receive this judgment because of his or her disobedience to God. God could no longer live with them because God is holy. This person also loved their sin more than they loved God. This person destroyed their temple by their own decisions and actions.

Do these verses give us more revelation on how God will judge?

> *These people are as useless as dried-up springs or as mist blown away by the wind. They are doomed to blackest darkness. They brag about themselves with empty, foolish boasting. With an appeal to twisted sexual desires, they lure back into sin those who have barely escaped from a lifestyle of deception. They promise freedom, but they themselves are slaves of sin and corruption. For you are a slave to whatever controls you. And when people escape from the wickedness of the world by knowing our Lord and Savior Jesus Christ and then get tangled up and enslaved by sin again, they are worse off than before. It would be better if they had never known the way to righteousness than to know it and then reject the command they were given to live a holy life. They prove the truth of this proverb: "A dog returns to its vomit." And another says, "A washed pig returns to the mud."* (2 Peter 2:17–22)

These verses describe former Christians who have become useless to Jesus Christ because they lure weak Christians back into sin with Satan's lies. They promise these weak Christians freedom because now they are free to do anything they want since they are now Christian. They refuse to declare the truth that they have been set free from the power of sin. Now they don't have to sin anymore because of the power of Jesus Christ in them. These people have become just like Satan when he twisted God's truth and made it into a lie in the Garden of Eden.

The fact is, these people love their sin and have become a slave to Satan once again. This all happened because they did not obey the command to live a holy life, and their punishment will be worse than for those who have never known Jesus Christ.

The question I have is, How many professing Christians are deceived, and will they be shocked at their judgment? Please,

please don't let it be you! You will either choose to believe the truth of God's Word or the lies of Satan and his advocates!

> *Stop deceiving yourselves. If you think you are wise by this world's standards, you need to become a fool to be truly wise. For the wisdom of this world is foolishness to God. As the Scriptures say, "He traps the wise in the snare of their own cleverness."* (1 Corinthians 3:18–19)

You have free will, and God will allow you to reject the leading of the Holy Spirit; then you will deceive yourself. How did you get the wisdom you have, and who gave it to you? When does the wisdom of this world have more authority than the Word of God? The world will call you a fool if you believe the Word of God over the ways and beliefs of the world. The wisdom of the world has been influenced by the lies of Satan! You can believe that you are so wise that you will actually begin to believe that portions of the Word of God are not true and you will refuse to believe it. You will be trapped in your own wisdom to believe Satan's lie, and as a consequence, your judgment will not go the way you thought. But it will be too late to change the result of God's decision. The time to establish what is truth in what you think is now! Is it not foolishness to think you have more wisdom than God, who created you?

As a human being, you can deceive yourself! You begin to shape your wisdom and make it conform to the wisdom of the world. This happens because you don't want to be different. You then begin to reject the wisdom of God, and you believe that you have found a way to please God *and* the world! Oh, how foolish!

> *And again, "The Lord knows the thoughts of the wise; he knows they are worthless."* (1 Corinthians 3:20)

The Lord knows every thought you have and declares they are worthless if they are not based on the truth of God's Word. Wisdom is studying the Word of God and allowing the Holy Spirit to give you divine revelation of the meaning, so you can understand and then apply it to your everyday life.

> *So don't boast about following a particular human leader. For everything belongs to you—whether Paul or Apollos or Peter, or the world, or life and death, or the present and the future. Everything belongs to you, and you belong to Christ, and Christ belongs to God.*
> (1 Corinthians 3:21–23)

Another area of deception that Satan uses is to get you to believe that you are not important in God's eyes. Remember, God created you for him. Once you believe in Jesus Christ, the Holy Spirit lives in you and gives you power to accomplish the work he has called you to do. All of this has been given so you can do your part in building God's kingdom. Your part in building the kingdom of God is just as important to God as anyone else's.

Don't allow Satan to get you to take your eyes off God. God is the One who has given you everything. Satan will try to get you to focus on a particular human leader instead of God. Do not put your faith in any human leader, only the Lord. The relationship between God and you is powerful because Satan has been defeated through Jesus Christ. All you need to do is put your faith, trust, and love in Jesus Christ. Never give up or go back to believing Satan's lies.

Because we are all building God's kingdom, we may be tempted to give glory and honor to a human being instead of God. We forget that God is the One who gives us our ministry (or calling), gives us the words to say, and everything that is accomplished is accomplished through the power of the Holy Spirit if we are obedient. We are to give all glory to God, not another human being. I am afraid that we give too much honor and glory to our fellow human beings instead of God.

When we are tempted to place a leader on a pedestal in our minds, we lose sight of who gave this person the calling to reach out to you. We lose sight of who gave this person the knowledge and gifts to help you grow. It was our Lord, and all glory goes to him.

Satan's trap is easy to fall into, and many have walked away from the Lord when their particular leader fell in disgrace.

This is about a personal relationship with our Lord Jesus Christ; we are to put our trust in him and only him. He gives us the Holy Spirit to direct our paths; he leads others to even help us. But the overriding fact is, no one has anything that hasn't been given to them by the Lord. And Jesus has made a commitment to you that everything he has belongs to you because you belong to him. So, everything you need to accomplish your calling will be given to you by our Lord Jesus Christ, if you seek him and not a particular human leader.

> *At this point many of his disciples turned away and deserted him. Then Jesus turned to the Twelve and asked, "Are you also going to leave?"* (John 6:66–67)

As Jesus was teaching his disciples, he taught them a truth that they would not believe or accept, and they gave up and did not follow him again. This teaching was so hard that Jesus asked the twelve disciples if they were going to leave as well.

Is there any part of God's Word that you find hard to believe and will not accept it as truth? I warn you: This is a tactic that Satan uses to defeat many who start the race and will not finish. Will you be one of them? Guard the Word of God in your heart and mind and just believe; don't doubt or be double-minded!

14

God Will Build His Kingdom on the Foundation of Love

The kingdom of God will be built on three pillars of love:

- God's love for human beings
- Human beings' love for God
- Human beings' love for other human beings

The First Pillar: God's Love for Human Beings
Here are a few verses that demonstrate God's love for human beings:

> *God saved you by his grace when you believed. And you can't take credit for this; it is a gift from God.*
> (Ephesians 2:8)

You were saved from death and separation from God when you believed in Jesus Christ. This grace is a gift made available to you because of God's love for his creation (you).

> *Salvation is not a reward for the good things we have done, so none of us can boast about it.*
> (Ephesians 2:9)

You can't say, "I received salvation because I was a good person and therefore deserved it or am entitled to salvation." Every human being was a sinner at birth, and the whole human race needed a Savior. From God's perspective and plan, now was the time to demonstrate to human beings his love and willingness to forgive them—if they believed in his Son, Jesus Christ. This provision was made available only to human beings and not to angels. At this time, God is revealing more of his characteristics to all of his creation.

> *For we are God's masterpiece. He has created us anew in Christ Jesus, so we can do the good things he planned for us long ago.* (Ephesians 2:10)

This establishes that God is an all-knowing God. Because God knew that Adam and Eve would fail the test, it had already been determined that human beings would have to be created anew in Christ Jesus. This proves to all of God's creation that the Lord is a master Creator. God has the love and the ability to mold and make human beings into what he wanted them to become, and we would be able to do the good things he planned for us to do. This plan was established even before the foundation of the world.

This plan included allowing human beings to choose whom they would serve because God's requirement was that all of his creation must be willing to submit to God's authority and believe in Jesus Christ. The power needed to accomplish these good things is given to us through the power of Jesus Christ and the Holy Spirit.

Please don't misunderstand what I am saying. It was not God's will that Adam and Eve sinned. Just because God knows everything before it happens does not mean that what happens is God's perfect will. After all, angels and human beings have been given free will. If you choose to obey Satan and serve him, it will be in spite of the love God has revealed to you.

The Second Pillar: Human Beings Must Love God

> *Jesus replied, "'You must love the Lord your God with all your heart, all your soul, and all your mind.' This is the first and greatest commandment."*
> (Matthew 22:37–38)

When this verse says that you must love the Lord your God, it doesn't leave any room for misunderstanding. This is the greatest commandment above all others that God has given to his creation.

How does God determine if you love him with all your heart, all your soul, and your entire mind? Do you love God this way?

> *"If you love me, obey my commandments."*
> (John 14:15)

God knows you love him when you do what he says. It's really that simple. So, if you don't obey his commandments, you are telling God through your actions that you don't love him.

> *But don't just listen to God's word. You must do what it says. Otherwise, you are only fooling yourselves.*
> (James 1:22)

It doesn't matter where the knowledge comes from; when you read and study the Word of God, or the Holy Spirit reveals to you what the Word says, you must obey. If you don't obey, you are only fooling yourself that everything is okay. Because if you continue down the road of disobedience, eternal destruction lies at the door.

Is a born-again Christian different from anyone else in the world? Is it possible that a born-again Christian can be deceived about his or her status with the Lord? What must you do?

> *So humble yourselves before God. Resist the devil, and he will flee from you.* (James 4:7)

The only way to humble yourself is to recognize that you need God's help in defeating your enemy (namely, Satan's influence in your life). When you ask God for his help, you can then resist the devil and he will flee from you. That is accomplished because of the power of the Holy Spirit in you.

The Third Pillar: Beings Must Love Other Human Beings

> *"A second [commandment] is equally important: 'Love your neighbor as yourself.' The entire law and all the demands of the prophets are based on these two commandments."* (Matthew 22:39–40)

How does God determine if you love your neighbor as yourself?

Let's consider the following verses.

> *"And forgive us our sins, as we have forgiven those who sin against us."* (Matthew 6:12)

When you ask God to forgive your sins (now), you must have already forgiven those who have sinned against you. You are giving God's love in you to your neighbor because you want to love like Jesus Christ and forgive others even when they don't deserve it. God is establishing a truth, that he loves the person who sinned against you as much as he loves you.

> *"And don't let us yield to temptation, but rescue us from the evil one."* (Matthew 6:13)

Now you are at a dangerous crossroads. You have a choice to obey God and forgive or yield to the temptation not to forgive. This temptation is a product of Satan himself. You must acknowledge that you have already been given the power to resist the devil.

However, God has allowed you to decide who you are going to serve and obey. You must allow the Holy Spirit in you to give you power to overcome the temptation of Satan, because your human free will does not want to forgive.

> *"If you forgive those who sin against you, your heavenly Father will forgive you."* (Matthew 6:14)

Never forget that your sin will be forgiven if and only if you forgive those who have sinned against you. God is declaring to you under what conditions he will forgive your sin. You can put your faith in God and know that he will forgive your sin when you have forgiven those who have sinned against you. Your testimony to others is the love of God given to others through you. When you are obedient to God, you will have peace in your heart and mind.

> *"But if you refuse to forgive others, your Father will not forgive your sins."* (Matthew 6:15)

If you yield to Satan's temptation, you are at a dangerous intersection. Let's look at what is occurring in your heart and mind. If you refuse to forgive others, you are rejecting the leading of the Holy Spirit and the Word of God. God determines the consequences for your willful disobedience to his Word.

How important is it to you that your sins are forgiven? Is this response evidence that you really don't love God? Do you believe this word of truth, or is it possible you have deceived yourself into believing that God understands and that you are justified in not forgiving?

When you refuse to forgive, you begin to believe (the original temptation) you can be like God. Don't fall into Satan's trap or lie. Lucifer's temptation to you is as follows: If someone sins against you, you make a judgment call (not God); you determine that they don't deserve forgiveness. In fact, you would be offended against God if one day that person accepted Jesus Christ and received salvation, because you believe they belong in hell for what they did to you. You certainly wouldn't do anything to try to reach out to them and win them to the Lord.

However, I believe the story doesn't have to end here. Let's consider 2 Peter 3:9 and 11:

> *The Lord isn't really being slow about his promise, as some people think. No, he is being patient for your sake. He does not want anyone to be destroyed but wants everyone to repent. . . . What holy and godly lives you should live.*

You are so blessed when God is patient with you instead of executing judgment on you, and then he gives you more time to repent as the Holy Spirit tries to encourage you to do what God has commanded.

So many professing Christians refuse to believe or accept that they can live a holy and godly life, because they deny the power that would enable them to actually do that. That power was given to them by the blood of Jesus Christ. Don't believe Satan's lie. You will decide if you are going to be a forgiving servant or a rebellious servant who needs more time to repent. However, if more time is given by God, it is limited; the longer you wait to obey, the harder it is to repent. Remember, God does not change.

> *If I could speak all the languages of earth and of angels, but didn't love others, I would only be a noisy gong or a clanging cymbal. If I had the gift of prophecy, and if I understood all of God's secret plans and possessed all knowledge, and if I had such faith that I could move mountains, but didn't love others, I would be nothing. If I gave everything I have to the poor and even sacrificed my body, I could boast about it; but if I didn't love others, I would have gained nothing.*
> (1 Corinthians 13:1–3)

These gifts are given to you by the Holy Spirit. This passage compares the importance of each gift to the gift of love. This comparison is from God's viewpoint! It is important to evaluate your love for others through God's eyes and not your own.

> *Love is patient and kind. Love is not jealous or boastful or proud or rude. It does not demand its own way. It is not irritable, and it keeps no record of being wronged. It does not rejoice about injustice but rejoices whenever the truth wins out. Love never gives up, never loses faith, is always hopeful, and endures through every circumstance.* (1 Corinthians 13:4–7)

Can you recognize God's love in you? Since God is perfecting us to become more like him, should we be more proactive and examine ourselves through the Holy Spirit's leading and conviction? Would we grow faster if we did this every day?

> *Prophecy and speaking in unknown languages and special knowledge will become useless. But love will last forever! Now our knowledge is partial and incomplete,*

> *and even the gift of prophecy reveals only part of the whole picture! But when the time of perfection comes, these partial things will become useless.*
> (1 Corinthians 13:8–10)

In the new kingdom of God, some gifts will no longer be needed, but the gift of love will be required in you forever!

> *When I was a child, I spoke and thought and reasoned as a child. But when I grew up, I put away childish things. Now we see things imperfectly, like puzzling reflections in a mirror, but then we will see everything with perfect clarity. All that I know now is partial and incomplete, but then I will know everything completely, just as God now knows me completely.*
> (1 Corinthians 13:11–12)

There is so much that you do not know or understand about God! These verses compare life for you today versus life on the other side, in the new kingdom (heaven). They also declare that God knows everything about you (right now), completely.

> *Three things will last forever—faith, hope, and love—and the greatest of these is love.* (1 Corinthians 13:13)

The number one attribute of those who are allowed to enter the new kingdom of God is their ability to love others the way Jesus does. Throughout eternity, as God reveals and implements each new plan, your love for God and what he is creating will never fail. Your faith in God will never end because you have put your faith in him. Your hope in God will never cease because you know that everything God does is for the benefit of his kingdom and you. You will be able to live in confidence that none of the redeemed will ever turn against God in the new kingdom!

Now is the time to allow God to perfect you into the person he wants you to become! It is your choice and decision if you are going to allow God to continue his work in you!

> *Dear friends, let us continue to love one another, for love comes from God. Anyone who loves is a child of God*

> *and knows God. But anyone who does not love does not know God, for God is love.* (1 John 4:7–8)

Love is the biggest battlefield on which you will wage war against Lucifer and all his advocates. The reality is that this battle never stops, and you must endure to the end. From God's viewpoint, if you don't love, you don't know God.

> *We know how much God loves us, and we have put our trust in his love. God is love, and all who live in love live in God, and God lives in them. And as we live in God, our love grows more perfect. So we will not be afraid on the day of judgment, but we can face him with confidence because we live like Jesus here in this world.* (1 John 4:16–17)

When you obey God, you have put your trust in his love and you will live in God, and then your love grows more perfect. How wonderful it will be for you on your judgment day when you are judged by a holy God, because the love of God is in you and you loved others as God loved you. It does make a difference how you live. Now is the time to examine yourself!

> *"Then the king called in the man he had forgiven and said, 'You evil servant! I forgave you that tremendous debt because you pleaded with me. Shouldn't you have mercy on your fellow servant, just as I had mercy on you?' Then the angry king sent the man to prison to be tortured until he had paid his entire debt.*
>
> *"That's what my heavenly Father will do to you if you refuse to forgive your brothers and sisters from your heart."* (Matthew 18:32–35)

This is how God looks at forgiveness as it relates to fellow human beings. The unforgiving servant (of God) is sent to prison to pay a debt that can never be paid. You have been forgiven for an unpayable debt, so let's not fall into the same trap that Lucifer or his advocates have set for us!

> *Most important of all, continue to show deep love for each other, for love covers a multitude of sins.* (1 Peter 4:8)

No matter what you experience from the actions of others, maintain a deep love for them, because some will be given more time to accept Jesus Christ, and when they do, God will forgive a multitude of sins. This is accomplished through the love of God in you.

> *"Don't sin by letting anger control you." Don't let the sun go down while you are still angry, for anger gives a foothold to the devil.* (Ephesians 4:26–27)

When you are unwilling to forgive, anger begins to control your actions. Your disobedience to God gives the devil a powerful foothold in your life. This anger will grow more powerful and control your life in many different ways. Never forget, unrepentant anger grows into hate, or spiritual murder, and could lead to physical murder. When you are bound by Lucifer's power or control, the only remedy is turning back to Jesus Christ.

How long can you wait before your unforgiving spirit and anger begin to control you? You have until the sun goes down or before you go to sleep. In your sleep, the devil can establish a strong foothold in your unrepentant heart and mind. It does not matter whose fault it is (in regard to the conflict). It is all about your witness of the love of Jesus Christ in you for that person who angered you. Anger changes the way you communicate and represent Jesus Christ to them.

You must always recognize that letting anger control you is sin! Satan wants you to feel justified in your anger and then wants you to pass judgment on the one who angered you.

Your love for that individual should be greater than your desire for revenge; leave the responsibility of judgment to God.

15

Examining the Belief of "Once Saved, Always Saved"

I want to examine the saying "once saved, always saved" from two schools of thought:

- From God's perspective
- From humans' perspective

First: From God's Perspective and Plan

From the beginning, God knew that human beings would never be able to overcome their free will and love God in their own power. So, it was determined, before the foundation of the world, that the Son of God would be given a human body, shed his blood on the cross, and die for all humanity.

When you believe in Jesus Christ as your personal Savior and allow him, through the power of the Holy Spirit, to begin the process of changing your life, you still have a choice to change your mind and perhaps decide, *I like my old lifestyle.* Jesus Christ will allow you to go back into bondage/slavery to Satan's power. Always keep in mind, God allowed Lucifer and the fallen angels to decide whom they were going to serve. They did, in fact, worship God in heaven (at one time), with all the benefits that came with that service.

> *I am convinced that nothing can ever separate us from God's love. Neither death nor life, neither angels nor demons, neither our fears for today nor our worries about tomorrow—not even the powers of hell can separate us from God's love. No power in the sky above or in the earth below—indeed, nothing in all creation will ever be able to separate us from the love of God that is revealed in Christ Jesus our Lord.* (Romans 8:38–39)

It's clear: The only power that can separate you from God's love is you. Not because God doesn't love you, but you have chosen not to love God of your own free will. God has given you free will, and you can change your mind and heart about your love for him. That can only happen if you refuse to believe and trust in God's power that can make you holy. This happens when you decide that you will no longer be obedient to the leading of the Holy Spirit and repent.

There should be no doubt of the great power you have been given because you believe in Jesus Christ, and your love, faith, and trust grow stronger in him day by day as you obey.

> *But you belong to God, my dear children. You have already won a victory over those people, because the Spirit who lives in you is greater than the spirit who lives in the world.* (1 John 4:4)

You must believe God's Word; it is the only truth you can depend on if you believe. It does come down to a couple of questions. Do you believe that the Holy Spirit lives in you? And do you believe that the Holy Spirit is greater than the spirit who lives in the world?

When you understand in your mind and heart that you belong to God, you have already won a victory over the people who don't belong to God, because they are controlled by the spirit of this world. With that knowledge, you have the power to overcome sin.

Why deny the power that can make you an overcomer over all the powers of this world? Please don't fall into Satan's deception that you can't overcome sin.

> *Anyone who continues to live in him [Jesus] will not sin. But anyone who keeps on sinning does not know him or understand who he is.* (1 John 3:6)

The statement *"Anyone who continues to live in him will not sin"* means you have a choice if you're going to obey and live in him. You must always believe, trust, and have faith in Jesus. Your actions are the evidence of who you serve. You must do what the Holy Spirit is saying to you and stop sinning because of your love for God. This verse also states that if a person continues to sin, they do not know Jesus or even understand who he is, and they have chosen to believe Satan's lies.

So, the truth is, if you live in Jesus, you will not continue to sin. Are you beginning to understand how much God has given you to overcome Satan's power? Everything!

> *The godly may trip seven times, but they will get up again.* (Proverbs 24:16)

A person who loves God may stumble, but he will listen to the Holy Spirit and get up again and repent. As he obeys the leading of the Holy Spirit, he grows stronger and he is able to overcome the power of sin. He does not give up because his love for God is steadfast.

> *So I say, let the Holy Spirit guide your lives. Then you won't be doing what your sinful nature craves. The sinful nature wants to do evil, which is just the opposite of what the Spirit wants. And the Spirit gives us desires that are the opposite of what the sinful nature desires. These two forces are constantly fighting each other, so you are not free to carry out your good intentions. But when you are directed by the Spirit, you are not under obligation to the law of Moses.* (Galatians 5:16–18)

This passage describes one of the things that the Holy Spirit does: guides your life. Remember, your sinful nature came from Satan, and evil are the actions that you produce when you refuse to allow the Holy Spirit to guide your life. You see, it is your decision whom you will serve.

Let's discuss the meaning of the last sentence of this passage. It states that when you do what the Holy Spirit directs you to do, you are not obligated to the law of Moses, because the Holy Spirit will never lead you to do evil.

The law of Moses was to reveal to human beings what is evil (sin) and given to us by Satan.

Another way to describe this situation is this: Evil is the fruit of Satan's character. The fruit of the Holy Spirit is love, joy, peace, patience, kindness, goodness, faithfulness, gentleness, and self-control, and there is no law against these things! You are free to possess all of these characteristics, absolutely free. Your actions are the evidence of who you serve. Let's consider 2 Timothy 3:14–17:

> *But you must remain faithful to the things you have been taught . . . You have been taught the holy Scriptures . . . and they have given you the wisdom to receive the salvation that comes by trusting in Christ Jesus. All Scripture is inspired by God and is useful to teach us what is true and to make us realize what is wrong in our lives. It corrects us when we are wrong and teaches us to do what is right. God uses it to prepare and equip his people to do every good work.*

The requirement for the body of Christ is to remain faithful and trust in the Word of God as the Holy Spirit reveals it to us.

Many professing Christians say it is not about doing good works. Every person is either working for God (good works) or for Satan (evil works). The Holy Spirit and the Word of God change the way you think, and will equip and empower you to do the good works that God has called you to do. So, you can't boast about the good works that you do, because everything needed to accomplish the good works has been given to you by God, including your calling. So, you can see that you still have a choice whether you will reject the power that could make you godly or refuse to allow the Holy Spirit to guide your life. The fact is, you will choose your eternal destination. After all, your actions are the evidence of who controls your life.

To summarize: God created you and made himself known to you through his Word, the Holy Spirit, and other born-again witnesses. So, God has demonstrated, beyond a shadow of a doubt, that he loves you. Now God wants you to love, obey, and worship him as your Creator in your free will.

God has given you everything you need to live a holy life, but he has also given you the freedom to reject his power to overcome Satan's lies and your sinful nature. God requires his creation to worship and obey him (only). That is why we must be tested and tried.

Who is God going to allow in his new kingdom? Only those angels who were obedient to God's authority and command, because they were given instruction on how to help his creation, human beings (namely, you).

> *And I remind you of the angels who did not stay within the limits of authority God gave them but left the place where they belonged. God has kept them securely chained in prisons of darkness, waiting for the great day of judgment.* (Jude 6)

Who is God going to allow in his new kingdom? Only those humans who love God and Jesus Christ and have learned to obey the leading of the Holy Spirit will ever occupy God's new kingdom.

Do you believe that God has given you everything you need to be an overcomer? Do you believe that God's power is greater than Satan and all his advocates? Will you overcome the power of sin in your life? It is now up to you; who are you going to serve with your free will?

The Second School of Thought from a (Fallen) Human Perspective

The core of this "once saved, always saved" belief is deceptive! This idea means a born-again Christian can lose his right of free will to serve God. In essence, God will take them to heaven even if they turn their back on Jesus Christ and continue to sin, without repentance, and they have lost their love for Jesus Christ.

Since Lucifer and his advocates have been defeated, they have only one option left. If they can successfully convince you to deny the power and work that have already been made available to you (to make you godly), you can once again become a slave to Satan's power. Just as Adam and Eve were tempted to reject the truth, you also will be tempted to reject the truth and believe his lie.

Let's look at some of the Scriptures that testify to the fact that you don't lose your free will. The people who adopt this belief (once saved, always saved) must reject the truth of God's Word, because they still have free will. Please allow the Holy Spirit to give you divine revelation of the truth in your own life.

> *They will act religious, but they will reject the power that could make them godly.* (2 Timothy 3:5)

This is a picture of professing Christians who act religious in our eyes but have rejected the power that will make them godly in their hearts and minds. You can't know what is in their hearts or minds—but God does.

Therefore, you must defend the faith, without doubt, and accept the power that you are given to live a godly life in your heart and mind. Your actions will be your testimony of the decision you made to live a godly life.

> *[I am] urging you to defend the faith that God has entrusted once for all time to his holy people. I say this because some ungodly people have wormed their way into your churches, saying that God's marvelous grace allows us to live immoral lives. The condemnation of such people was recorded long ago, for they have denied our only Master and Lord, Jesus Christ.* (Jude 3–4)

You must always defend the faith that God has already entrusted to you, being one of his holy people.

Let's examine what these two verses reveal.

This is from God's viewpoint, on how he evaluates this teaching. The professing Christians in this passage (our viewpoint) tell others that God's marvelous grace allows you to continue sinning and still be saved. Many professing Christians say that when you are born again, you are forgiven of all your sins—past, present, and future. This is the concept of "once saved, always saved". If that were true, there would be no need to ever repent after being born again. These people declare that you can continue sinning as before and live just like the world and God's grace will cover your sin.

Who could these ungodly people be? They are in the church.

Some could be leaders in authority, ministers, teachers, lay members, and so on. They now reject the truth of God's Word and even deny the only master and Lord, Jesus Christ, in their hearts and minds.

This Scripture gives you an insight into God's ability to know the future before it happens, and God's judgment or condemnation has been recorded long ago. You see, God will allow these individuals to deny and turn away from Jesus Christ, and allow them to become slaves to Satan again.

While these individuals are telling you that God's grace covers your sin, the Holy Spirit is convicting you of your sin and trying to get you to repent and turn from your wicked ways.

Who should you listen to? The consequences to the person who is teaching you the opposite of what the Holy Spirit is saying to you can be eternal—if that person doesn't repent and start speaking the truth of God's Word. Never forget, Jesus Christ came to do away with sin, not take it to heaven in you.

> *So I want to remind you, though you already know these things, that Jesus first rescued the nation of Israel from Egypt, but later he destroyed those who did not remain faithful.* (Jude 5)

This verse establishes how important it is to God that you remain faithful! Will you remain faithful to God, or will you turn your back on him and believe a lie? If you don't remain faithful to God, he will destroy you, because he never changes.

> *What sorrow awaits them! For they follow in the footsteps of Cain, who killed his brother. Like Balaam, they deceive people for money. And like Korah, they perish in their rebellion.* (Jude 11)

What could motivate a person to lie about the truth of God's Word? There are several motives. Let's look at three examples.

Cain. Why did he kill his brother, Abel? First, Cain wanted to worship God in his own way through his sacrifice. Do you want to worship God in your own way? Second, Cain knew God's requirement for an animal sacrifice. Third, Abel obeyed God in his sacrifice, and Cain refused to obey God's command in his sacrifice.

Fourth, Cain hated God but took out his hatred on Abel because his brother obeyed God and God accepted Abel's sacrifice. After all, what could Cain do to God? The only thing Cain could do to God was refuse to obey God's command and kill Abel, his brother, who did obey God. In today's society, how often do you see people exhibit hatred toward those who obey God's Word?

Balaam. Who was Balaam? Balaam had access to God. But Balaam was motivated by money and followed Satan's example on how to tempt the Jews to sin. If you can get God's people to sin, then they could no longer be blessed by God. As a result of their sin, they would be cursed by God (Revelation 2:14). How many ministers, teachers, and so on will alter the truth of God's Word for money and prestige? Many once taught the truth of God's Word but stopped following the leading of the Holy Spirit so they could get a greater following and increased revenue. What unknown sorrow awaits people who have compromised the truth of God's Word and refused to give people the opportunity to repent of their sin.

Korah. Who was Korah? Korah rebelled against Moses and Aaron, who were given authority by God to lead his people (Numbers 16:1–4). This story reveals the consequences of people who rebel against the authority of God's chosen leaders. They actually rebelled against God; Moses and Aaron were the recipients of their rebellion. They never recognized the influence that Satan had on their thinking process.

As we study Korah, we see that he was not called by God to remove Moses and Aaron from the authority that God had given them. However, we can see the consequences that Korah and his followers received because of their actions.

How many times has a person gone against the authority of a minister/pastor without the leading of the Holy Spirit? The consequences of that action will be eternal, because it can destroy the love of God in the hearts and minds of many people.

All authority is given by God: the president, leaders, police, and so on. When people try to overthrow them, they are actually rebelling against God. Their judgment will be eternal because they usurped God's authority.

> *He controls the course of world events; he removes kings and sets up other kings.* (Daniel 2:21)

We must never forget that God gives a person authority to accomplish his will or purpose. When it is time to remove them from that position, God removes them. God determines how that removal is accomplished. God will be the judge if that person did his will or not.

To realize this fact—that I have the potential to give counsel to someone that is different from the counsel the Holy Spirit is giving them—is heart-wrenching. I don't ever want to be on that side of the equation for any reason. I should only say what the Holy Spirit tells me to say to any human being.

To summarize: I recognize that my life is a testimony to others by the way I live and the words that I declare. I have come to an understanding in my life that if I declare to a person that I can't live a holy life, I am actually denying the power that can make me godly. I am even planting a seed of doubt in their mind. I realize that I may sin, but if I do, the Holy Spirit will convict me of my sin. It is my responsibility to listen to the Holy Spirit and repent, then turn from my wicked ways. Then, through the power of the Holy Spirit, I can be an overcomer. You see, I will never be able to accuse God and say that his power is weaker than the power of the flesh or the power of Satan or his advocates. Is that not open rebellion and teaching a lie? Also, do I become a false teacher or a liar if I declare to others that they have not been given the power to stop sinning?

I never want to become a false teacher or a liar!

> *For it is impossible to bring back to repentance those who were once enlightened—those who have experienced the good things of heaven and shared in the Holy Spirit, who have tasted the goodness of the word of God and the power of the age to come—and who then turn away from God. It is impossible to bring such people back to repentance; by rejecting the Son of God, they themselves are nailing him to the cross once again and holding him up to public shame.* (Hebrews 6:4–6)

These verses state that once you are born again, there can come a point in your life where you can reject the Word of God and the leading and correction of the Holy Spirit. This passage describes the consequences of this rejection, and you can no longer be reached so you can repent. You see, you have rejected the only power, Jesus Christ, that can change the way you live and think.

I believe that if you reach this point in your life, you no longer want anything to do with God. You may still go to church, but you just go through the motions of being a Christian. You have allowed Satan to deceive you into believing that everything is all right. That is what it means that you are spiritually dead. The world sees you as no different from them, and they see no need to become a Christian. Your testimony and influence to them become a public shame. Only God knows when you reach this point.

> *Dear friends, if we deliberately continue sinning after we have received knowledge of the truth, there is no longer any sacrifice that will cover these sins.*
> (Hebrews 10:26)

Once you are born again, you receive the Word of God in your heart and mind; the Holy Spirit reveals the truth of God's Word to you and how to apply it to your life. Your desire should be to love God and to become like Jesus Christ.

However, Satan begins trying to convince you that you don't have to give up all the sin in your life because God wants you to have fun, and he will still love you in your sin.

This is a dangerous crossroads that you will face. When you sin, the Holy Spirit will convict you of your sin. If you deliberately continue sinning even after you received the knowledge of the truth from the Holy Spirit, or any of the advocates of Jesus Christ, the end result is your spiritual death and separation from God.

God still loves you; however, God is holy, and he gives you an opportunity to repent and reject what Satan is telling you. The decision is yours; you will either follow the lead of the Holy Spirit or follow Satan and keep on sinning.

Jesus Christ is the sacrifice that was given to cover your sins, and there is no other sacrifice acceptable to God. Jesus Christ came to do away with sin in your life, not to allow it to continue in your life. If you die in this state, you have sealed your fate.

> *"Anyone who speaks against the Son of Man can be forgiven, but anyone who speaks against the Holy Spirit*

> *will never be forgiven, either in this world or in the world to come."* (Matthew 12:32)

When you are born again, you receive the Holy Spirit. That is when your relationship with Jesus Christ begins, through the Holy Spirit. The Holy Spirit starts to communicate to you what Jesus Christ has already told the Spirit to tell you. The Holy Spirit is the vehicle of communication between Jesus Christ and you. When you speak against what the Holy Spirit is telling you to do, you are rejecting the Spirit that was given to you to lead you into holiness. If you die in that state, that ultimate sin can never be forgiven, in this world or the world to come.

Speaking against the Holy Spirit is accomplished through your words and actions by continuously rebelling against the Holy Spirit and not obeying his council so you can do the will of God in your life.

> *When you follow the desires of your sinful nature, the results are very clear: sexual immorality, impurity, lustful pleasures, idolatry, sorcery, hostility, quarreling, jealousy, outbursts of anger, selfish ambition, dissension, division, envy, drunkenness, wild parties, and other sins like these. Let me tell you again, as I have before, that anyone living that sort of life will not inherit the Kingdom of God.* (Galatians 5:19–21)

You should know that your sinful nature came from Lucifer. I often look at it like this: All human beings are born with Lucifer's DNA, bent toward rebellion. Ever since the fall of Adam and Eve, his characteristics have been found in every human being except Jesus Christ. Jesus Christ came to break the power of Satan and his DNA that flows through the hearts and minds of all human beings. If only human beings would believe in Jesus Christ, they would be given the power to obey his Word and defeat the power of their enemy, Satan.

Galatians 5 is declaring who will not inherit the kingdom of God or, in other words, will not go to heaven.

Those who will not inherit the kingdom of God include everyone who refuses to believe in Jesus Christ and accept the power that was made available to be an overcomer over sin. The number of people who fall into this category is mind-boggling.

Those who will not inherit the kingdom of God also include professing Christians who refuse the leading of the Holy Spirit, and they revert back to Satan's characteristics and actions in their lifestyle. They will have already lost their first love for Jesus Christ, and their ability to hear the Holy Spirit can be seared, as with a hot iron.

The reality is, all human beings who refuse to believe in Jesus Christ and obey him will have as their final destination hell and are separated from a loving God for eternity. What a sad reality for those who choose to reject God's offer, because God had created them for a special purpose and calling.

I need to make this clarification: When I use the terminology "professing Christians," this does not mean all of them have separated themselves from their relationship with Jesus Christ. God determines how much more time he is going to give you to repent.

Again, the choice is yours, until God determines your time to repent has run out.

> *You should know this, Timothy, that in the last days there will be very difficult times. For people will love only themselves and their money. They will be boastful and proud, scoffing at God, disobedient to their parents, and ungrateful. They will consider nothing sacred. They will be unloving and unforgiving; they will slander others and have no self-control. They will be cruel and hate what is good. They will betray their friends, be reckless, be puffed up with pride, and love pleasure rather than God. They will act religious, but they will reject the power that could make them godly. Stay away from people like that!* (2 Timothy 3:1–5)

These verses describe a period of time that affects the body of Jesus Christ. The passage is a description of professing Christians who revert back to Satan's control.

You can look around you and see all these characteristics being displayed, even from professing Christians, and you see it every day.

Why would a Christian give up on the love of God and go back to his sinful nature?

The reason this happens is because human beings reject the power that could make them godly, which was made available to them through the Holy Spirit.

Unbelieving human beings think the things of God are foolishness.

As you can see from these Scriptures, you never lose the right of free will to choose who you are going to serve and obey, God or Satan.

> *Look to God's instructions and teachings! People who contradict his word are completely in the dark.*
> (Isaiah 8:20)

This verse clearly establishes that you should understand the importance of reading God's Word for yourself. Knowing the Word of God gives you direct knowledge, so you recognize the lie when someone contradicts the Word of God. God's Word is the only authority that you can put your whole trust in.

People who are in the dark are controlled by Satan because he brings spiritual darkness to the individuals who will listen.

So, it is up to you to know the truth.

I believe the perfect Scripture that illustrates your responsibility is Acts 17:11:

> *And the people of Berea were more open-minded than those in Thessalonica, and they listened eagerly to Paul's message. They searched the Scriptures day after day to see if Paul and Silas were teaching the truth.*

Has Satan closed your mind to reading the Word of God in search of the truth? Look at our society today, and all of man's interpretations of the Word of God. God is the interpreter of his Word through the Holy Spirit. The question is, How important is it to you to know the truth? Do you examine God's Word to see if what you are being taught is the truth?

Even as I write these pages, you should examine this book in light of God's Word. That is why I have established the importance of giving you so many Scriptures to help you consider the truth. Please allow the Holy Spirit to give you divine revelation and understanding of God's Word. There is power in the Word of God. The more you study, the stronger you become, so you can accomplish what God has called you to do.

So many people have closed their minds to the Word of God. Will you be one of them? Your decision is so important to your final and eternal destination.

16

Judgment of the Body of Christ

For the time has come for judgment, and it must begin with God's household. And if judgment begins with us, what terrible fate awaits those who have never obeyed God's Good News? And also,

> *"If the righteous are barely saved,*
> *what will happen to godless sinners?"*

So if you are suffering in a manner that pleases God, keep on doing what is right, and trust your lives to the God who created you, for he will never fail you.

—1 Peter 4:17–19

Let's examine some Scriptures that reveal the Lord's view on the statement that judgment begins in God's household. I realize that the Holy Spirit is the only One who can reveal truth to us. So, let's submit our hearts and minds to the truth of the Word of God through the Holy Spirit.

Always remember that God gave you his Word and he revealed the truth to you. God will hold you accountable to his Word in his judgment of you. My interpretation of the Word of God, or other interpretations, must match God's truth—or your understanding is meaningless. You are absolutely dependent on the Holy Spirit's divine revelation to you.

Never forget, Lucifer has been altering the truth of God's Word in the minds of human beings for a long time, and he is good at it.

When you accepted Jesus Christ as your Savior (when you were born again), you entered into the household of faith and you began your journey to become like Jesus—and everything began to change in your life. The Holy Spirit reveals the Word of God that has been planted into your heart and mind. The next step for you in this process is reading God's Word. The Holy Spirit will give you divine revelation and understanding so you will know how to live your life in obedience to Jesus Christ. As you obey, you will grow stronger in the Lord and in his mighty power. Once again, you will decide if you like the lifestyle change!

Is there anything that you can learn from Revelation chapters 2 and 3 (Jesus Christ's judgment of the churches/individuals in the church)?

As you study these chapters, keep in mind that you are an active participant in this examination. What is the Holy Spirit revealing to you that you must change?

Revelation: Chapters 2 and 3

In Revelation chapters 2 and 3 is an example of how Jesus Christ judged seven churches of that day. The number *seven* means completeness, which means none are forgotten or overlooked. So, what does that have to do with you? These chapters describe how Jesus Christ has examined every church and individual since his resurrection, and that continues today. As Jesus Christ examines you, he tells the Holy Spirit what to say to you. Now, you will decide if you are going to listen to the Holy Spirit, or even have an ear left to hear what the Holy Spirit is saying to you. The realization for you is to listen to what the Spirit is saying to you today and every day. Always remember that Lucifer and his advocates are on a constant mission to alter the truth of the Word of God, which can change your understanding or mind. The question is, Will you obey what the Holy Spirit reveals to you?

Jesus Christ examines everything you do. He reveals to the Holy Spirit what you are doing right and what you need to strengthen. He understands your suffering and trials and identifies the characteristics that must be corrected through his power. The Holy Spirit reveals everything to you. Your opportunity to repent will usually last until you die. And you know that you are not guaranteed tomorrow. Once you die, repentance is not an option.

Consider this: Judgment or correction actually begins here on earth while you are still alive and still have an opportunity to change the outcome!

All Seven Churches Receive This Admonition

> *"Anyone with ears to hear must listen to the Spirit and understand what he is saying to the churches."*
> (Revelation 2:7, 11, 17, 29; 3:6, 13, 22)

Please don't get caught in the cycle of procrastination! Are you listening to what the Holy Spirit is saying to you? Is your hearing tuned to the voice of the Holy Spirit?

If you love God and you want to be victorious, you do not have the option to ignore what the Spirit is saying to you. Your decision is a matter of life and death.

Again, the question is, Will you listen to the counsel of the Holy Spirit and repent and turn back to following Jesus Christ? It is certainly your choice and decision to make.

The sad reality for many in the church is they have rejected the leading of the Holy Spirit for so long that they no longer hear what the Spirit is saying to them.

The Examination of Revelation 2 and 3 Begins

Each of the seven churches received encouragement for the things they were doing right.

Here are some of the things they were doing in the churches that were correct:

They worked hard with patient endurance, didn't tolerate evil people, examined the claims of those who said they were apostles but were not, discovered liars, and patiently suffered without quitting.

Jesus told some of these Christian, in essence, "You have remained faithful and loyal to me, refused to deny me; you've remained faithful in your witness, obeyed my Word, expressed your love, your faith, your service, and experienced constant improvement in all these things."

How important is it to you that you have these same characteristics?

You can exhibit these same characteristics through the power of Jesus Christ.

Remember, not everyone in these churches demonstrated these actions. Each individual was examined by Jesus Christ.

The churches also received complaints that must be corrected. Here are some of the complaints that existed in the churches that needed to be corrected.

They lost their first love of God and each other, committed sexual sin, worshipped idols, tolerated false teaching, and had a reputation for being alive—but they were spiritually dead. Jesus found that their actions did not meet the requirements of God; they were liars, neither hot nor cold; believed that they were rich, that they didn't need a thing—even God.

But they didn't realize how wretched and miserable and poor and blind and naked they were.

Let's remember Jesus Christ is examining individuals in the church who started their journey obeying him. With trials and tribulations and Satan's temptation, they begin to disobey the Holy Spirit's counsel. God still loves these people, and the Holy Spirit is still trying to get these people to repent and come back to God.

You may ask, "Where are these people headed if they refuse to repent?" For as an example, we already know all liars go to hell. The first and second commandment is that you must love God and each other. If you refuse to love God and others, your new home will be hell, along with all the other sinners. The statement "I find that your actions do not meet the requirement of my God" is sobering. Jesus knows what God requires in those who are going to heaven, and these people don't meet that requirement, so their destination is hell if they don't repent.

Remember, not everyone in these churches demonstrated these actions. Each individual was examined by Jesus Christ.

Here were the consequences if they refused to repent:

> *"If you don't repent, I [Jesus] will come and remove your lampstand from its place among the churches."*
> (Revelation 2:5)

Here Jesus states that he will remove his light from you if you don't repent. If you don't go to heaven, the only other destination is hell. You are called to be a light to your world of influence.

> *"Repent of your sin, or I will come to you suddenly and fight against them with the sword of my mouth."* (2:16)

We can see that sin in a Christian is a serious problem. The Word of God is the sword that will be used at judgment time. The whole human race will be judged by it. I am afraid that many Christians have become complacent to sin.

> *"I gave her time to repent, but she does not want to turn away from her immorality. Therefore, I will throw her on a bed of suffering, and those who commit adultery with her will suffer greatly unless they repent and turn away from her evil deeds."* (2:21–22)

God gives you time to repent, so take hold of your free will and repent. Don't allow your love for sin to control you.

> *"And I will give to each of you whatever you deserve."* (2:23)

If you turn your back on Jesus Christ and refuse to repent, you deserve spiritual death and eternal separation from God.

> *"Repent and turn to me again. If you don't wake up, I will come to you suddenly, as unexpected as a thief."* (3:3)

This describes a person who is continuously sinning and is spiritually asleep.

> *"I will . . . erase their names from the Book of Life."* (3:5)

If you are not victorious over your love of sin, your name will be erased from the Book of Life. You were given the power to be an overcomer of sin, and the only thing standing in your way is your free will. What will be your decision? You see, your name has to be in the Book of Life to be erased. Consider everything God has done for you!

Exodus 32:30–35 describes how God looks at disobedience to his law and the individuals who sinned against him after everything he had done for them.

At the end of Exodus 32, something important is revealed. Moses acknowledged that God was keeping a written record of the names of his chosen people and then asked God to forgive their sin or erase his name (Moses) from God's written record. God stated to Moses that his name would not be erased from his written record, only those who had sinned against him (God). I believe there is a truth here that God is revealing to us even today.

If you once again believe Satan's lie and turn your back on God's Word, even after God has given you Jesus Christ as your Savior and the Holy Spirit to reveal truth to you and make him known to you in your everyday life—the consequences of your unbelief and rejection are that your name will be erased from God's written record, because God will not violate your decision.

You must never forget that God is the same yesterday, today, and forever, and allow the Holy Spirit to reconcile that truth in your heart and mind.

> *"I will spit you out of my mouth!"* (Revelation 3:16)

This describes a person who is in Jesus Christ but is lukewarm and believes everything is okay and remains spiritually apathetic. They will not allow Jesus Christ to be Lord of their life and serve him only.

Receive advice from the Holy Spirit! Obey!

> *"Look how far you have fallen! Turn back to me and do the works you did at first."* (2:5)

This is more evidence of the role the Holy Spirit has in your life and the importance of obeying! You are counseled to examine yourself and turn back to Jesus Christ, and your actions of love toward others will follow.

> *"Don't be afraid. . . . Remain faithful."* (2:10)

Don't be afraid what other people will say or do to you. Obey the Word of God and the counsel of the Holy Spirit. Don't give up.

Reject the teaching of false teachers.

This is a dangerous area. You will come across false teachers who will alter the truth of God's Word. That is why it is so important to know the Word of God, because the truth of God's Word will set you free from the power of the lie of false teachers.

> *"[Understand] that I am the one who searches out the thoughts and intentions of every person."* (2:23)

The moment you recognize the Holy Spirit has the power to understand even your hidden thoughts and intentions is when you will begin to obey his counsel. You can't hide anything from God.

Reject false teaching ("deeper truths," as some call them, from the depths of Satan, actually).

Again, false teaching is described (2:24), and the passage declares where this teaching is actually coming from: Satan. I believe that most of the false teachers don't even recognize where this lie is coming from. So, believe the Word of God, and the Holy Spirit will reveal the lie of Satan to you.

> *"Obey me to the very end."* (2:26)

This states that you must obey to the end of your life. You must finish the race and be faithful.

What does it mean to be a *"faithful witness"* (2:13)? To always show the love of Jesus Christ to everyone, your friends *and* enemies.

> *"I can see your constant improvement in all these things."* (2:19)

Now that you have begun this journey of being a servant of Jesus Christ, you are constantly learning how to love, think, and speak. You are learning this from the Word of God and the counsel of the Holy Spirit. Along this journey you may stumble and fall, but your love and desire to obey mean that you will repent and get back up and follow the counsel of the Holy Spirit. This process means you will grow stronger day by day and constantly improve until the day God calls you home. Through the power of the Holy Spirit, you will sin less and less, and you will be an overcomer of the power of your free will.

> *"Repent of your sin."* (2:16)

This establishes the importance of repentance in your life. You have been given an opportunity that fallen angels will never be given, and that is to repent. You are given the opportunity to come back to the Lord Jesus Christ. To *repent* means to stop committing the sin and to obey the counsel of the Holy Spirit.

> *"Wake up!"* (3:2)

So many have fallen asleep and they are not aware of their spiritual situation. Please examine yourself to see if you are still in the faith.

> *"Strengthen what little remains, for even what is left is almost dead."* (3:2)

It is because Jesus loves you that he gives you his counsel through the Holy Spirit to alter the judgment of God regarding you. He gives you the truth of where you stand with him, whether you like it or not. It is now up to you to take action so that you don't die (spiritually).

> *"Go back to what you heard and believed at first; hold to it firmly."* (3:3)

It is important to remember the truth that you heard when you first believed in Jesus Christ. Hold on to that truth, and don't believe Satan's lies.

> *"You obeyed my word and did not deny me. . . . You have obeyed my command to persevere."* (3:8, 10)

You must believe and obey God's Word because if you don't, you are actually denying Jesus Christ. Only you can determine if you are going to obey God's command and persevere through all the trials and tribulations that come your way to make you stronger in Christ Jesus.

> *"You are neither hot nor cold. I wish that you were one or the other!"* (3:15)

If you're hot, it means Jesus Christ is the Lord of your life. If you're cold, it means that Jesus Christ is not Lord of your life. However, if you are cold, it is easier for the Holy Spirit to draw you back into a right relationship with Jesus Christ than it is if you are lukewarm, or spiritually indifferent.

> *"Buy gold from me—gold that has been purified by fire. . . . Also buy white garments from me . . . and ointment for your eyes."* (3:18)

What does it mean to "buy from" Jesus? I believe that when you love God, obey the Word of God, and obey the counsel of the Holy Spirit, you're purchasing your white garments and ointment for your eyes, through your obedience.

Another verse that helps in understanding this is Revelation 19:8:

> *"She has been given the finest of pure white linen to wear." For the fine linen represents the good deeds of God's holy people."*

How important is it to you to bring your free will into the obedience of the leading of the Holy Spirit? You will receive your white garment because your obedience to God produces good deeds.

> *"I correct and discipline everyone I love."* (3:19)

This statement lets you know that because Jesus Christ loves you, he is faithful to correct and discipline you when needed. At your judgment, you will never be able to accuse God and claim that you didn't know what you needed to do or didn't know that you needed to repent for your sins.

> *"Look! I stand at the door and knock. If you hear my voice and open the door, I will come in, and we will share a meal together as friends."* (3:20)

This describes Jesus standing outside of your heart and trying to get back in. Will you welcome Jesus back into your life? The Holy Spirit is giving you, as a professing Christian, counsel about your life in Christ Jesus. Have you ever examined how easy it is to ignore the leading of the Holy Spirit in your own life?

There is a reward for those who are victorious over Satan.

How important is it to you to be victorious in God's eyes? What will be the consequences to you if you are not victorious in God's eyes? What do you have to be victorious over?

> *"To everyone who is victorious I will give fruit from the tree of life in the paradise of God."* (2:7)

If you are victorious, Jesus Christ will give you fruit from the Tree of Life. This Tree of Life was removed from the Garden of Eden so that Adam and Eve were not allowed to eat from it. What a privilege to be able to eat the fruit from the Tree of Life. I believe we don't understand the importance of being able to eat this fruit from the Tree of Life!

Where will you spend eternity if you are not victorious over Satan through the power of Jesus Christ?

> *"But if you remain faithful even when facing death, I will give you the crown of life."* (2:10)

This describes the importance of remaining faithful to God even when you are facing death. Then you will be given the crown of life. You must have the crown of life to be in heaven.

> *"Whoever is victorious will not be harmed by the second death."* (2:11)

The second death is not when you die a physical death. The second death is if you are separated from God in hell because of your unrepentant heart and your obedience to Satan and his lies.

> *"To everyone who is victorious I will give some of the manna that has been hidden away in heaven. And I will give to each one a white stone, and on the stone will be engraved a new name that no one understands except the one who receives it."* (2:17)

At this time, you don't understand the importance of the manna that was not made available to eat on this earth. When you are given a white stone with your new name, it reveals a personal love relationship that God has with you, all because of your love and obedience to him.

> *"To all who are victorious, who obey me to the very end, to them I will give authority over all the nations. They will rule the nations with an iron rod and smash them like clay pots. They will have the same authority I received from my Father, and I will also give them the morning star!"* (2:26–28)

This describes the importance of obeying Jesus to the end of your physical life. Being given authority to rule over all the nations with a rod of iron occurs during the one-thousand-year reign of Jesus Christ. This authority may extend even into eternity. Do you understand that if you are victorious, you will be given the same authority that Jesus Christ received from God?

> *"All who are victorious will be clothed in white. I will never erase their names from the Book of Life, but I will announce before my Father and his angels that they are mine."* (3:5)

This states that you must be victorious to be clothed in white. So many refuse to believe that it is even possible that a person's name could ever be erased from the Book of Life. Will you be victorious so that Jesus Christ can announce to God the Father and his angels that you are one of his (Jesus Christ's), one of the redeemed?

> *"Because you have obeyed my command to persevere, I will protect you from the great time of testing that will*

> *come upon the whole world to test those who belong to this world. I am coming soon. Hold on to what you have, so that no one will take away your crown."* (3:10–11)

When you continue to love God and others even during the hard times, Jesus will protect you from the great tribulation. If Jesus is not Lord of your life, you will have to go through the great tribulation because Satan and the world is your lord. The last sentence of this passage shows that it is possible for your crown to be taken away if you don't hold on to your belief in Jesus Christ.

> *"All who are victorious will become pillars in the Temple of my God, and they will never have to leave it. And I will write on them the name of my God, and they will be citizens in the city of my God—the new Jerusalem that comes down from heaven from my God. And I will also write on them my new name."* (3:12)

If you are not victorious, you will not receive these blessings. What an honor to be recognized by God as a pillar in his temple. What a profound relationship of love that Jesus has for those who obey him. You will never have to leave his temple because you will always obey him for eternity.

> *"Those who are victorious will sit with me on my throne, just as I was victorious and sat with my Father on his throne."* (3:21)

What an honor to be able to sit with Jesus Christ on his throne.

> *"All who are victorious will inherit all these blessings, and I will be their God, and they will be my children."* (21:7)

Is it important to you that you are victorious over all of Satan's lies so that you can receive all the blessings God has prepared for you? Why do so many refuse to believe it is necessary to be victorious over Satan?

Where do you stand in your relationship with Jesus Christ? The only power that can deny you these blessing is your free will. Your decision will determine where you spend eternity.

SECTION 4

Jesus Christ Rules for One Thousand Years

17

Jesus Christ Rules for One Thousand Years

Then I saw an angel coming down from heaven with the key to the bottomless pit and a heavy chain in his hand. He seized the dragon—that old serpent, who is the devil, Satan—and bound him in chains for a thousand years. The angel threw him into the bottomless pit, which he then shut and locked so Satan could not deceive the nations anymore until the thousand years were finished. Afterward he must be released for a little while.

—Revelation 20:1–3

After the tribulation, a dramatic change in the plan of God occurs. Why is Satan confined to the bottomless pit during the thousand-year reign of Jesus Christ? Why is Satan released after the thousand years for a little while to deceive the people of the world?

I will address these questions from a different perspective: How does free will impact the outcome of the thousand-year reign of Jesus Christ? But first let's establish the situation at the beginning of the millennium.

We know that part of the reason is to fulfill God's covenant with the Jewish people. We also know that only people who did not take the mark of the beast entered into the millennium with

Jesus Christ and his army (the redeemed believers who came to rule and reign with him on this earth).

> *Then I saw an angel standing in the sun, shouting to the vultures flying high in the sky: "Come! Gather together for the great banquet God has prepared. Come and eat the flesh of kings, generals, and strong warriors; of horses and their riders; and of all humanity, both free and slave, small and great."*
>
> *Then I saw the beast and the kings of the world and their armies gathered together to fight against the one sitting on the horse and his army. And the beast was captured, and with him the false prophet who did mighty miracles on behalf of the beast—miracles that deceived all who had accepted the mark of the beast and who worshiped his statue. Both the beast and his false prophet were thrown alive into the fiery lake of burning sulfur. Their entire army was killed by the sharp sword that came from the mouth of the one riding the white horse. And the vultures all gorged themselves on the dead bodies.* (Revelation 19:17–21)

Scripture is clear that only the people who did not receive the mark of the beast are allowed to enter the millennium. God knows the reason why these people did not take the mark of the beast—just because they did not take the mark of the beast does not make them believers in Jesus Christ.

The beast (the Antichrist) and the false prophet are cast into the lake of fire of burning sulfur. They have received their physical and spiritual judgment at the same time.

Satan's direct influence convinces the world leaders and armies they can defeat Jesus Christ and his armies. However, at the least, he will be instrumental in accomplishing his number one goal, and that is to kill and destroy as many human beings as possible. Satan wants to separate humanity from the love relationship they could have with God if only they would surrender to the King of kings. They witness Jesus Christ with his armies coming down from the heavens—and still believe they can defeat him. Once a person starts believing Satan's lies, that deception is powerful on their hearts and minds. And if they don't believe in Jesus Christ or his Word, there is no hope for them in their unbelief.

Every human being who accepted the mark of the beast physically dies. Their judgment for the works they did on earth, done for ungodly reasons, occurs later, at the great white throne judgment. That judgment determines the severity of their punishment.

Jesus Christ and his army (the redeemed believers who came to rule and reign with him on this earth) can be physically seen by the human beings in this time frame. This fact highlights the huge difference between now (living by faith) and then actually seeing and hearing from Jesus Christ in person.

Jesus Christ executes judgment on the world by himself, and his army (the redeemed) watches in amazement. What absolute power and authority Jesus Christ displays as he takes his rightful place as King of all kings and Lord of all lords. The redeemed become firsthand witnesses of the consequences to human beings who are disobedient to God's commands and laws. This knowledge is important to the redeemed as they obey Jesus and carry out their assignment that he has given them. They will rule and reign with Jesus Christ, all the generations of human beings who will live during those thousand years.

> *"To all who are victorious, who obey me to the very end,*
>
> *To them I will give authority over all the nations.*
> *They will rule the nations with an iron rod*
> *and smash them like clay pots.*
>
> *They will have the same authority I received from my Father, and I will also give them the morning star!"* (Revelation 2:26–28)

These verses describe the redeemed who obeyed Jesus to the end of their physical lives. Jesus Christ will give the redeemed their roles and responsibilities that they will have during the thousand-year reign with him. The human beings who did not take the mark of the beast will still have free will to worship Jesus Christ as their Lord. However, I believe that most of them will not obey the laws that Jesus Christ establishes during this time frame, and these laws will be no different from now. And this disobedience will occur *without* the direct influence of Satan! However, Satan's indirect influence will still remain, evidenced in acts such as worshipping other gods, lying, and all the others ways to disobey the commands of Jesus Christ, because of the way they were taught.

I believe God proves to all his creation when they have been given free will to serve and obey him that it is difficult for them to control their human nature without the power of Jesus Christ and the Holy Spirit.

What does it mean that the redeemed will rule the nations with a rod of iron and smash them like clay pots? Will Jesus give them (the redeemed) the same authority that was given to him by God?

Jesus Christ was given all authority and power to accomplish God's plan. At this time, the redeemed (which includes the martyrs who would not take the mark of the beast) will be given the same authority and power to accomplish the plan of God. Here is only some of the authority they will have: controlling the weather, executing punishment, giving out blessings, and so on. Ruling with a rod of iron and smashing them like clay pots does not sound like the description of a wonderful time for the people who will not obey the laws and teachings of Jesus Christ. All of this is done to get these human beings to willingly submit and obey the authority of Jesus Christ.

Now, what does it mean that Jesus will give all who are victorious the morning star?

> *Until the Day dawns and Christ the Morning Star shines in your hearts.* (2 Peter 1:19)

I believe this is the time frame when you as a redeemed person will be given the complete mind of Christ to think the way he thinks, to love the way he loves, to forgive the way he forgives, and to punish people of this world with the same punishment that he would execute.

> *We are human, but we don't wage war as humans do. We use God's mighty weapons, not worldly weapons, to knock down the strongholds of human reasoning and to destroy false arguments. We destroy every proud obstacle*

> *that keeps people from knowing God. We capture their rebellious thoughts and teach them to obey Christ. And after you have become fully obedient, we will punish everyone who remains disobedient.*
> (2 Corinthians 10:3–6)

I believe these verses describe your life as a redeemed believer in two stages. The first stage of your life is the here and now, when your ability is limited because you are being perfected by Jesus Christ and the Holy Spirit. To say it another way, you are learning to be like Jesus Christ, learning to love others like he does, and learning to forgive others like he does.

The question I will ask is, Are you willing to allow the Holy Spirit to perfect you, and are you willing to obey?

The second stage is during the thousand-year reign with Jesus Christ, when you are fully obedient to Christ. But your new responsibility then will be to wage a spiritual war for the hearts and minds of human beings in a way that is hard to even imagine now. At that time, part of your responsibility will be to reprimand human beings who remain disobedient to Christ's laws, and this will be accomplished through the mind of Jesus Christ.

> *So prepare your minds for action and exercise self-control. Put all your hope in the gracious salvation that will come to you when Jesus Christ is revealed to the world.* (1 Peter 1:13)

This verse describes your responsibility to prepare your mind and exercise self-control right now. Your actions will determine how far along you are in accomplishing God's will. This will prepare you for your reign with Jesus Christ during the thousand years when he is revealed physically to the world.

> *But when the time of perfection comes, these partial things will become useless.* (1 Corinthians 13:10)

When is the *"time of perfection"*? I believe the time of perfection occurs when we come back with Jesus Christ to rule and reign with him during the thousand years. The things you have been given now in this physical life are prophecy, speaking in unknown languages, and special knowledge—these gifts will become useless.

> *When I was a child, I spoke and thought and reasoned as a child. But when I grew up, I put away childish things.* (1 Corinthians 13:11)

In your physical body, you are like a child, and you are being taught by the Holy Spirit. If you obey the Holy Spirit, the way you speak to someone and the way you think and reason in your mind begin to change, and you begin the process of growing up in spiritual knowledge and understanding.

> *Now we see things imperfectly, like puzzling reflections in a mirror, but then we will see everything with perfect clarity. All that I know now is partial and incomplete, but then I will know everything completely, just as God now knows me completely.* (1 Corinthians 13:12)

In your physical body, you don't see things as God sees them, but you are learning to obey the leading of the Holy Spirit. The time frame when you will see with perfect clarity is when you are given the mind of Jesus Christ at his return, to rule and reign a thousand years.

> *Three things will last forever—faith, hope, and love—and the greatest of these is love.* (1 Corinthians 13:13)

This verse establishes three characteristics that the body of Jesus Christ will possess for eternity. You will never lose your faith, hope, and love in Jesus Christ regardless of the plans he has for you to accomplish throughout eternity. God has determined that love is the greatest characteristic you will exhibit.

> *Everyone will live in peace and prosperity,*
> *enjoying their own grapevines and fig trees,*
> *for there will be nothing to fear.*
> *The LORD of Heaven's Armies*
> *has made this promise!*

> *Though the nations around us follow their idols,*
> *we will follow the* Lord *our God forever and ever.*
> (Micah 4:4–5)

This occurs during the thousand-year reign of Jesus Christ. Human beings will be given the opportunity to live in peace and will prosper under the rule of Jesus Christ. They will be able to decide whether or not they will submit to his authority and obey his laws. They will be taught the Lord's ways and be able to worship him.

During this time frame, what does *peace* mean? The Lord and his armies will rule with a rod of iron and will not allow war to occur between countries and nations. Today we pray for peace so our children don't have to go to war. Throughout history, millions of people have been killed in war after war because Satan's objective was to get us to kill each other by any means possible. However, this does not mean everyone will have peace in their hearts and minds, because not everyone will love God's laws or decisions. Jesus will enforce peace during the thousand years. Again, what people do with their free will determines where they will spend eternity.

Jesus Christ will prove to all his creation the importance of submitting to his authority and teaching. The only way any kingdom can survive is to obey him in everything they do. They must recognize that his way is the best for them. It is so important that when they know the truth, they must bring their free will into captivity and obey his laws and statutes and commands.

The last part of this verse answers an important question: No one in the Lord of heaven's army will ever deny or disobey Jesus again. Jesus's armies will bring their free will under the authority of the Lord their God because they have promised to follow him forever and ever. And since God is all-knowing, he knows if that is the truth.

The next truth we find out is that human beings will be allowed to worship their idols without Jesus eliminating them. Jesus teaches them through his armies who he is and then allows them to change their free will and believe in him as the only true God. The worship of idols is the indirect influence Satan had on the world before he was bound during these thousand years.

It is amazing—the people of this world and time frame will see Jesus with their physical eyes and witness his judgments and recognize they are just, yet many will still refuse to worship him as the only true God.

Will you be one of the warriors in the army of Jesus Christ who will commit to serving him forever and ever? To get this opportunity, you must now be faithful and never give up.

> *In the last days, the mountain of the LORD's house*
> *will be the highest of all—*
> *the most important place on earth.*
> *It will be raised above the other hills,*
> *and people from all over the world will stream there to worship.*
> *People from many nations will come and say,*
> *"Come, let us go up to the mountain of the LORD,*
> *to the house of Jacob's God.*
> *There he will teach us his ways,*
> *and we will walk in his paths."*
> *For the LORD's teaching will go out from Zion;*
> *his word will go out from Jerusalem.*
> *The LORD will mediate between nations*
> *and will settle international disputes.*
> *They will hammer their swords into plowshares*
> *and their spears into pruning hooks.*
> *Nation will no longer fight against nation,*
> *nor train for war anymore.* (Isaiah 2:2–4)

Jerusalem will become the most important place on earth, and Jesus Christ will rule from there. People from all over the world will come to worship and be taught by Jesus so they will be able to walk in his paths. All people in the world will understand that Jesus Christ is the greatest power on earth.

But for many, their free will will control their actions, and it will require Jesus to mediate between nations and settle international disputes. All instruments of war will be destroyed so they can't accomplish the murderous desires of their hearts. The indirect influence of Satan (his DNA) will still reside in the hearts and minds of human beings unless they are obedient to follow the ways of Jesus Christ.

Satan's imprisonment in the bottomless pit is important to the plan of God. It is Satan's desire to kill all human beings because he hates God and human beings are created in his image. Satan will accomplish this goal through war, murder, abortion, infanticide—just to name a few ways.

Do you think that Jesus will allow women with free will to abort and kill their babies, whom God has created? I believe that the so-called right of a woman to kill her unborn child will not be allowed. This conflict in the free will of human beings will be another area of animosity toward following the ways of Jesus Christ.

I believe that every child born during this time period will have the right to live and learn about Jesus Christ so they will have the opportunity to freely serve and worship him.

The fact that it is necessary for Jesus to settle disputes means somebody's free will and desire will not go their way. This is just one of many ways that animosity toward Jesus Christ will build over one thousand years. Every human being will have to make a decision on whether or not they will submit to the authority of Jesus Christ and bring their free will under his authority.

> *"The thief 's [Satan's] purpose is to steal and kill and destroy. My [Jesus's] purpose is to give them a rich and satisfying life."* (John 10:10)

If Satan were allowed to deceive human beings during the thousand-year reign of Jesus Christ, then human beings would not be able to witness and experience the rich and satisfying life that Jesus would give them. With Satan imprisoned in the bottomless pit, Jesus Christ will be able to demonstrate the difference between his rulership and Satan's tyranny.

> *Satan, who is the god of this world, has blinded the minds of those who don't believe.* (2 Corinthians 4:4)

This is another reason for Satan's imprisonment, so that all human beings will be able to see and experience everything about Jesus Christ. They will be able to experience the blessing when they obey and the punishment when they refuse to obey. Everyone will make a decision with their own free will regarding whom they are going to worship, serve, and obey: Jesus or their sinful nature. The decision to worship Satan will come at the end of the thousand years, when Satan is released from the bottomless pit to deceive the world again.

The next set of Scriptures will describe the thousand-year reign of Jesus Christ from God's perspective. God will establish that Jesus Christ is his Son and that he has given him the throne in Jerusalem to rule from God's holy mountain. God will give advice to the inhabitants of the earth. God will also describe the attitude of the human beings; some will serve with reverent fear and submission, and then some will be angry with Jesus Christ and plot together to break away from his rule.

> *For the Lord declares, "I have placed my chosen king on the throne in Jerusalem, on my holy mountain."*
> (Psalm 2:6)

God will make the declaration that he has chosen Jesus Christ to be king and to rule from Jerusalem.

> *The king proclaims the LORD's decree: "The LORD said to me, 'You are my son. Today I have become your Father.'"*
> (Psalm 2:7)

Jesus Christ will proclaim to the inhabitants of the world that God has decreed that he (Jesus) is the Son of God and God is his Father.

Here is a side-note regarding the plan of God established before the foundation of the world:

- That Jesus Christ would be given a human body
- That Jesus Christ (the Word) would be the sacrifice for the sins of humanity
- That Jesus Christ would have to be tested and tried (by Satan)
- That Jesus Christ would have to be obedient to God the Father in all his ways and be without sin, and that was accomplished

When Jesus Christ was faithful to God the Father, it justified to all of God's creation the title *Son of God.*

Before, God executed all judgment as he willed.

The structure and the relationship of the Godhead changes.

Now, Jesus Christ will mediate with God the Father on behalf of the believers as they grow in the mighty power of Jesus Christ.

God will still determine the length of time that must be completed before the next phase of his plan is executed.

God will give Jesus Christ the power and responsibility to teach and execute judgment on all living human beings for one thousand years.

God will execute the final judgment of angels and all mankind from the beginning of time.

> *"Only ask, and I will give you the nations as your inheritance, the whole earth as your possession."* (Psalm 2:8)

Because Jesus Christ was obedient to God the Father in accomplishing every aspect of God's will, Jesus will rule the nations and be given the whole earth as his possession for his inheritance. God will never die (so that the inheritance can be passed along); he will only give a reward to Jesus Christ for his obedience to him.

> *"You will break them with an iron rod and smash them like clay pots."* (Psalm 2:9)

Here the psalmist describes what it will take to rule humanity with free will. The human beings who rebel against Jesus Christ and his authority will not be on a joyride. Jesus Christ will execute judgment and punishment from his own righteousness.

> *Now then, you kings, act wisely! Be warned, you rulers of the earth! Serve the Lord with reverent fear, and rejoice with trembling.* (Psalm 2:10–11)

The psalmist warns the kings and rulers of the earth to serve Jesus Christ with reverent fear and rejoice with trembling. He is describing the difference between judgments postponed (in today's society) versus immediate judgment and punishment for disobedience to his laws and commands.

> *Submit to God's royal son, or he will become angry, and you will be destroyed in the midst of all your activities—for his anger flares up in an instant. But what joy for all who take refuge in him!* (Psalm 2:12)

Submit means to obey Jesus Christ, the Son of God. If you disobey Jesus, he will become angry, and judgment will be executed immediately, which may result in physical and spiritual death. But for those who take refuge in Jesus, they will see what real justice looks like.

> *Why are the nations so angry? Why do they waste their time with futile plans? The kings of the earth prepare for battle; the rulers plot together against the* Lord *and against his anointed one.* (Psalm 2:1–2)

Because so much of humanity will not control their free will and submit to the rulership of Jesus Christ, their anger will grow. The anger will not be limited to just the leaders and kings, but will include the inhabitants of these nations. All of them who can't control their free will and submit to Jesus Christ will be part of the plot to destroy Jesus Christ and the God who made Jesus ruler over them.

It is important to recognize that humanity's inability to control their free will and submit to the authority of Jesus Christ will lead to anger. After all, Jesus Christ will be physically seen then. Humanity will witness the love, patience, justice, judgments, and power of Jesus Christ firsthand. And yet so many will reject his leadership and will not obey him because they have chosen their free will over their obedience to their Creator.

You need to understand that this all happens without the direct influence of Satan.

So, are you able to understand the importance of humanity with free will being tested and tried?

> *"Let us break their chains," they cry, "and free ourselves from slavery to God."* (Psalm 2:3)

How strong is your free will in your life? Are you able to control your free will and live by God's laws and still love him? Do you believe the yoke of Jesus is easy to bear and the burden he gives you is light? Or have you come to the point in your life where you feel like you are bound by chains and a slave to God?

People who are alive during Christ's millennial reign will know in their hearts what sin is because they will have been taught, but their free will will want to live life by their own desires. It will have such a power over them that they will actually plot how to overthrow the rulership of Jesus Christ, even after Jesus had demonstrated his power over them, and they will refuse to obey his laws and will not love him or his leadership.

Jesus will prove that he has the power and knowledge of how to rule humanity who will not obey him, but he will love them with an everlasting love to give them an opportunity to change their minds and serve him. Jesus will continue to try to convince them to submit to his authority for one thousand years. Then their opportunity will end, and their time of visitation will be complete.

What is next in God's plan is to release Satan from the bottomless pit and allow him a short time to deceive the nations of the world. Satan will convince them that if they follow him, they will be able to overpower Jesus Christ and his armies, and they will be able to live the way they want to live.

Malachi 3

Malachi 3 is another chapter that describes the events of the thousand-year reign of Jesus Christ; however, I will only highlight a few of the verses.

> *"At that time I will put you on trial. I am eager to witness against all sorcerers and adulterers and liars. I will speak against those who cheat employees of their wages, who oppress widows and orphans, or who deprive the foreigners living among you of justice, for these people do not fear me," says the Lord of Heaven's Armies.* (v. 5)

Jesus Christ will take an active role in revealing to humanity that he knows all things and nothing is hidden from his knowledge. No longer will judgment be postponed, but it will be executed immediately. Rebels will find out that though at one time their sins were secret from all humanity, now they are revealed and made known, and then judgment follows. At this time, humanity will know the laws that they are governed by but refuse to obey them because they don't fear the Lord. They will justify their sin because they enjoy the fruits of their free will.

> *"Then all nations will call you blessed, for your land will be such a delight," says the Lord of Heaven's Armies."* (v. 12)

During this time frame, Jesus will call the Jewish people to repentance. When they do repent, Jesus will bless their land and everything they do. The nations will witness this transformation and call them blessed. After seeing the result of the Jews' obedience to Jesus Christ, the nations will have to decide if they are going to obey Jesus Christ as well. Jesus Christ will be in the process of revealing himself to all of humanity so they can decide if they will serve this same Lord and reject their idols.

> *Then those who feared the Lord spoke with each other, and the Lord listened to what they said. In his presence, a scroll of remembrance was written to record the names of those who feared him and always thought about the honor of his name.* (v. 16)

Do you fear the Lord? I believe it is the fear of the Lord that motivates you to bring your free will into captivity in obedience to Jesus Christ. The next question is, Do you honor his holy name in everything you do and say? How important is it to you that your name be recorded in the book of remembrance? It is important to remember that God will allow things to occur that only he knows why, but your response is critical to maintain your love for him. There is no difference in how Jesus Christ will judge humanity now versus during the thousand-year reign. He is the same yesterday, today, and forever.

> *"They will be my people," says the Lord of Heaven's Armies. "On the day when I act in judgment, they will be my own special treasure. I will spare them as a father spares an obedient child."* (v. 17)

It is important to remember that all of humanity is created by God and for him. However, only obedient children will be spared and enjoy the fruits of that obedience.

> *"Then you will again see the difference between the righteous and the wicked, between those who serve God and those who do not."* (v. 18)

Will you be one of the righteous and obedient servants? You see, at the time of judgment, it will already be too late to change your status or destination.

> *When the thousand years come to an end, Satan will be let out of his prison. He will go out to deceive the nations—called Gog and Magog—in every corner of the earth. He will gather them together for battle—a mighty army, as numberless as sand along the seashore. And I saw them as they went up on the broad plain of the earth and surrounded God's people and the beloved city. But fire from heaven came down on the attacking armies and consumed them.* (Revelation 20:7–9)

When God determines that humanity's opportunity to commit to their love for Jesus and obey him is over, he will have Satan released from his prison. God will allow Satan to unite those who refuse to love and obey Jesus Christ with the sole purpose to destroy Jesus and his armies.

When these armies come against Jesus and his armies, Jesus will not ask God the Father to forgive them (because they don't know what they are doing). Their opportunity will be over, and they will have made their decision with their own free will. They will know exactly what they're doing.

This also illustrates the absolute deception Satan will have over humanity. All who are consumed by fire will be killed physically and will await the next part of God's plan, the great white throne judgment.

> *Then the devil, who had deceived them, was thrown into the fiery lake of burning sulfur, joining the beast and the false prophet. There they will be tormented day and night forever and ever.* (Revelation 20:10)

God will execute judgment on Satan, the devil, and he will receive his reward for eternity. Now that this time frame is complete, the next phase of God's plan will begin.

> *For the LORD has crushed your wicked power and broken your evil rule. You struck the people with endless blows of rage and held the nations in your angry grip with unrelenting tyranny.* (Isaiah 14:5–6)

These verses describe why God will execute his judgment on Satan. These verses also state that Satan will be behind all of this destruction of humanity. This is what Satan has done with his free will. What will you do with your free will?

18

The Great White Throne Judgment

Now that the preceding part of God's plan is complete and all humanity has made their final decision regarding who they are going to serve, the last and final judgment will take place.

The moment a person dies, the first judgment is determined. When a person refuses to believe and obey Jesus Christ, they are sent to a place of torment until the great white throne judgment. This is called the first death.

When a person believes and obeys Jesus Christ, they go to be present with the Lord. They await the Bema seat judgment, where they will be judged for their works and deeds. The Bema seat judgment occurs during the seven-year tribulation.

The great white throne judgment is about God judging the deeds and works of humanity going all the way back to the beginning of humanity. The main recipients at this judgment are the percentage of humanity who refused to obey God's laws and serve Jesus Christ. I believe there will be some who will believe and obey Jesus Christ during the thousand-year reign, but few by comparison at this judgment.

> *"But all who reject me and my message will be judged on the day of judgment by the truth I have spoken."*
> (John 12:48)

The purpose of this judgment is to judge those who rejected Jesus Christ and determine the severity of their punishment, which will last forever and ever. They will be judged by the Word of God—not by what humanity thinks—and his Word never changes.

> *And I saw a great white throne and the one sitting on it. The earth and sky fled from his presence, but they found no place to hide. I saw the dead, both great and small, standing before God's throne. And the books were opened, including the Book of Life. And the dead were judged according to what they had done, as recorded in the books. The sea gave up its dead, and death and the grave gave up their dead. And all were judged according to their deeds.* (Revelation 20:11–13)

For the first time, these people will come into the presence of their Creator and holy God. They will witness the earth and the sky fleeing from God's presence. This passage describes the absolute fear and desire to hide from their Creator. This fear comes upon the people who have rejected Jesus Christ and the provision that was made available so they could have fellowship with the Trinity. The books that will be opened will reveal the works that these people did while they lived. The books will also establish the truth of what they did for all to witness, and nothing will be hidden anymore.

It does not matter where or how they died; they will stand before their Creator and give an account of what and how they lived their lives.

I believe that when Scripture says "*death and the grave gave up their dead,*" it represents two demonic angels who are in charge of their captives. The captives encompass all who rejected Jesus Christ and would not obey God's laws.

How can anyone declare that it doesn't matter what they do or how they live? Scripture is clear: Everyone's works and deeds will be judged. And that includes you and me!

> *Then death and the grave were thrown into the lake of fire. This lake of fire is the second death. And anyone whose name was not found recorded in the Book of Life was thrown into the lake of fire.* (Revelation 20:14–15)

Death and the grave (demonic angels) will be thrown into the lake of fire along with the beast, the false prophet, and the devil, and they will be tormented day and night forever and ever.

Once the judgment is complete, anyone whose name was not found recorded in the Book of Life will be thrown into the lake of fire. There will be no names added to the Book of Life as a result of this judgment. Their fate will already be set in stone, and God's total plan as it relates to human beings will now be complete. God will have revealed to all of his creation (angels and humanity) every aspect of who he is. God will have revealed his holiness, his love, his righteous judgment, his mercy, his grace and empowerment, his forgiveness, and so many more attributes too numerous to name.

I believe that the angels never understood everything about the Trinity they worshipped and served. But by this point, through God's plan, the angels and all humanity will have experienced everything about the Trinity and the absolute power and wisdom that he displayed to all of his creation.

19

So, What Is God's Overall Purpose and Plan?

God is proving to all his creation that only he can rule his creation righteously, and they must be willing to recognize that he is the only authority to obey.

Today, God is allowing human beings to establish every kind or type of government, ruling body, authority, and even anarchy. This will prove to all his creation that no created being can rule and reign righteously. So, the evidence of this fact is the total rebellion to all authority throughout history. God is also allowing Satan and his fallen angels to influence humanity to establish every kind of authority that is against God's will.

God will allow this rebellion to go on until the last person accepts Jesus Christ as their Savior.

Let's look at the evidence before us today! Has there been any man or woman past or present with the ability to rule mankind with all of God's attributes?

Soon Lucifer will be allowed to rule this world through the Antichrist for seven years. We know some of what is going to happen in prophecy (Daniel and Revelation). Lucifer's desire to be worshipped as God will lead him to begin to force man to worship him as God or be killed! Yet most of mankind will not repent of their wicked ways or their murder or their witchcraft or their sexual immorality or their thefts—which establish and prove their allegiance to Lucifer.

> *Since we are receiving a Kingdom that is unshakable, let us be thankful and please God by worshiping him with holy fear and awe.* (Hebrews 12:28)

I believe the whole purpose in allowing all of this to happen is about God's desire to have a unique relationship with his creation. As God reveals himself to his creation, they will love and obey him as they love others. God wants his creation to submit their free will to his authority. After all the trials and the testing that every person will go through, the end result will be an unshakable kingdom. You must be thankful for what God is doing in perfecting you and getting you ready for his kingdom.

Establish the importance of worshipping God with holy fear and awe in your heart and mind. Satan and his advocates will always try to get you to forfeit your prize or crown. While you are alive on this earth, you will not understand the purpose of the trials or tribulations that you will go through, but put your faith and hope in Jesus Christ. He will finish the work he has started in you if you don't give up.

> *Whenever the living beings give glory and honor and thanks to the one sitting on the throne (the one who lives forever and ever).* (Revelation 4:9)

The four living beings will give glory and honor and thanks to the One sitting on the throne by declaring to all of God's creation, "Holy, holy, holy is the Lord God, the Almighty, the one who always was, who is, and who is still to come." They will do this day after day and night after night. This declaration will be heard by all of God's creation.

> *The twenty-four elders fall down and worship the one sitting on the throne (the one who lives forever and ever). And they lay their crowns before the throne and say, "You are worthy, O Lord our God, to receive glory and honor and power. For you created all things, and they exist because you created what you pleased."*
> (Revelation 4:10–11)

The twenty-four elders represent all of the redeemed of humanity, who now live in the new kingdom. The crowns will be given to them by God and represent the authority and honor they have been given. They will willingly acknowledge before God and his creation that God is the One who is to receive glory and honor and power. And the glory and honor and power that they have been given by God will never come between God and them. They will follow the lead of the four living beings and make this declaration day after day and night after night. They will also acknowledge that they were created by God and they exist because of God's sovereign will—and no other reason.

As for me, I am thankful that God created me and gave me the opportunity to choose to accept him as my Savior, to love him and serve him, and to be a part of building his kingdom! What a privilege!

> *Therefore, God elevated him to the place of highest honor and gave him the name above all other names, that at the name of Jesus every knee should bow, in heaven and on earth and under the earth, and every tongue declare that Jesus Christ is Lord, to the glory of God the Father.* (Philippians 2:9–11)

No other created being will ever receive the highest glory, honor, and power that Jesus Christ will be given by God. Throughout human history, God has given authority and power to kings and rulers of this world. Not one king or ruler will be able to love and rule God's creation like Jesus Christ will. It does not matter the position you had in this life. You will bow before the King of kings and Lord of lords, Jesus Christ. And I believe that includes all angels as well. And for most of humanity, it will be the first time they will declare that Jesus Christ is Lord, and all of this is for the glory of God the Father.

> *"Look, God's home is now among his people! He will live with them, and they will be his people. God himself will be with them."* (Revelation 21:3)

Finally, God is able to live with his new creation in the new Jerusalem. What a joyous time!

I do believe the redeemed will rule and reign with Jesus Christ in the new heaven and the new earth. I also believe that God is not done creating, and we have no idea what is in store for us throughout eternity. In the end, only the redeemed will put their trust and hope in Jesus Christ and God the Father.

I also believe that since the redeemed have already been tested and tried, there is no fear that anyone will turn against God the Father, Jesus Christ, and the Holy Spirit, as Lucifer and the fallen angels did in the beginning. Also, the Holy Spirit will never leave this new creation, those who make it to heaven.

20

Review of God's Plan for His Kingdom Through the Transition of Time

Why did God wait so long before he allowed Jesus Christ to come on the scene to give redemption to human beings and to one day establish his kingdom and rule over all of his created beings?

Since God determined to give angels and human beings free will and did not create them as robots, it is necessary to test them all. And through this process, God will build and establish his kingdom. Only those angels and human beings who will willingly love and obey God and accept his authority will be allowed in this new kingdom. All others will be separated from God and will exist in torment for eternity.

God revealed his laws to his chosen people (the Jews) because Satan's influence and lies had overpowered humanity. All of God's creation was a witness of the chosen people attempting to do what God had commanded yet failing time after time. Then they reverted back to Satan's lies. The next step, they began to openly rebel against God's laws and then demanded to be ruled by an earthly king. The purpose was to reveal to all his creation that the only way to redeem humanity was for Jesus Christ to come to forgive and then to give power to those who would accept and obey him. God would decide when it was time to reveal this mystery of the appearance of Jesus Christ to the world.

Even today, it is a mystery to me how God re-creates us in a way that changes the way we think and the way we live. Everything begins to change, including our desires and our willingness to forgive others. Our love for God grows deeper day by day as we study God's Word and obey the leading of the Holy Spirit.

> *This message was kept secret for centuries and generations past, but now it has been revealed to God's people. For God wanted them to know that the riches and glory of Christ are for you Gentiles, too. And this is the secret: Christ lives in you. This gives you assurance of sharing his glory.* (Colossians 1:26–27)

I believe one of the reasons why God waited so long before sending his Son, Jesus Christ, to this earth was to prove to all his creation that this was the only way that humanity could ever overcome their free will, and that they must freely accept this gift.

Do you really comprehend what it means that Jesus Christ lives in you spiritually—today, right now—and that it's your responsibility to obey? This gift of God's love was extended to all of humanity, if only they would believe and obey him.

Also, the work of perfecting those who believe in and obey him takes time. God's plan included you being a witness of his love to others—that also takes time for you to grow in his power and might. You can't do anything without Jesus Christ.

> *For we are God's masterpiece. He has created us anew in Christ Jesus, so we can do the good things he planned for us long ago.* (Ephesians 2:10)

Have you ever considered that you are God's masterpiece, a work of art or a novel in progress? Do you understand the importance of being created anew in Christ Jesus and how that affects the way you live and the way you think?

You were created with the knowledge and understanding that God is real, and he has put in your heart what is right and wrong. All around you, you witness the results of those who rebel against God's laws and commands. Then you realize you need a Savior and the godly power to overcome your free will and Satan's influence in the way you think and live.

Ephesians 2:10 also declares an important fact: Before God

created Adam and Eve, he knew you as well and had planned good things for you to do and accomplish—but because of Satan's intervention, you were not able to overcome Satan's influence with your own free will. That means even before the foundation of the world, God already knew that he would have to sacrifice his Son, Jesus Christ, and make you anew in Christ Jesus and give you his power so you can do the good things that he had planned for you to do.

I don't know if I will ever understand God's foreknowledge of everything. God's ability to know the future and then know what to do to give us the opportunity to freely receive him and his power so we can submit to his authority without taking our free will away is amazing to me.

The next phase of God's plan is quickly coming upon this world, and that is the tribulation, or the rule and reign of the Antichrist for seven years. The fact is, for many, the opportunity to change their eternal destination is coming to an end.

God loves you, and he wants you to be part of his new kingdom.

Will you love God and others as he has loved you? Will you set your affections on him and follow the leading of the Holy Spirit? Can you see the spiritual war that is occurring before your eyes, or have you been blinded by Satan's deception and his advocates? Are you living a lie as a slave to Satan's power?

Do not deny the power of Jesus Christ that you have been given to overcome Satan's lies and do the good things that God had planned for you to do, even before time as we know it began.

Your time is running out, and your opportunity to be a witness of Christ to others is going to come to an end.

Never forget studying God's Word, and your prayer life, because it determines how fast you grow in his power and how strong you become.

I believe not only did Adam and Eve and all humanity come to know the knowledge of good and evil, but angels are learning the same truth. Simply put, evil is disobeying God! Humanity and angels are learning the consequences of their disobedience to their Creator.

What a huge difference between human beings since Adam and Eve and human beings who have been created anew in Christ Jesus.

The world wants to deny that there is any spiritual difference (Satan's lie).

21

The Reality of the Spiritual Battle in Today's Society

This phase of God's plan, to offer humanity the opportunity to live in his kingdom of love through his patience, is quickly coming to a close.

Our society today refuses to believe that there are two spiritual forces (that you can't physically see) that affect the thinking of all humanity, which is revealed in the things they say and their actions in their day-to-day living.

> *Dear friends, do not believe everyone who claims to speak by the Spirit. You must test them to see if the spirit they have comes from God. For there are many false prophets in the world.* (1 John 4:1)

This verse is speaking to born-again Christians. It identifies two spirits, the Spirit from God and the spirit from Satan.

It identifies a major problem in your journey of living for God. It warns you to always test what is spoken to you by a professing Christian or anyone else. The spirit of Satan is subtle and can influence your friends to speak a lie or try to alter your calling. Don't forget, Satan spoke through Peter trying to convince Jesus Christ to alter his call to die for all humanity. Satan is speaking through human advocates today trying to get Christians to compromise God's Word in their own lives and in our society.

Have you ever considered that everything spoken (by anyone, including you) is from one of the two spiritual forces?

If that is true, is it important to examine what you say to people in every situation? How often have you said something and you wondered where it came from or wish you hadn't said it?

Consider these verses.

> *"And I tell you this, you must give an account on judgment day for every idle word you speak. The words you say will either acquit you or condemn you."*
> (Matthew 12:36–37)

You will decide the truth of those two statements in your own life.

How do you test what human advocates say to you, whether it is true or not? Whatever is spoken to you, if it is in conflict with the Word of God, it is a lie from Satan or his advocates. Make sure you don't ignore the counsel of the Holy Spirit. The Holy Spirit will never guide you against the Word of God!

It is important to understand and acknowledge that God keeps a record of everything you say. If what you declare is not from him (God), then it is from Satan or his advocates, and you become a false prophet. This has become a sobering revelation to me. At my judgment, I don't want my words to condemn me!

Our society today has been deceived in believing that Satan has no influence in our world today! How naive we have become!

> *Satan, who is the god of this world, has blinded the minds of those who don't believe. They are unable to see the glorious light of the Good News. They don't understand this message about the glory of Christ, who is the exact likeness of God.* (2 Corinthians 4:4)

Spiritual Blindness

Our society today has been overtaken by spiritual blindness, and the evidence is all around us. The cares of this world rule our thinking process, and we have come to think that it doesn't matter what we believe. In the verse above, what does it mean that Satan is the god of this world? It means that God has allowed

Satan to influence humanity to test them and see if they are willing to serve God instead of serving Satan. How can we deny the hate that we see exhibited every day in our society, and then deny that Satan had no influence in that hate?

What does it mean that Satan has blinded the minds of those who refuse to believe? It means that Satan has influenced their minds into thinking that his answer is the right way to deal with any situation. However, Satan's motive is to steal, kill, and destroy. Satan's objective is to steal the good things that God has given them. I believe that Satan's number one objective is to kill humanity by any means. The next area that Satan can influence is to get them to destroy the call that was given to them by God when they were created. In this spiritual blindness, they can become Satan's advocates, and their fruit will become the same as his. Satan cannot make them do any of these things. You will choose whom you will serve and obey.

The next part of this verse describes the consequences of this spiritual blindness. They are unable to see the glorious light of the good news. This good news reveals Jesus Christ and the power to overcome Satan's influence in our everyday living. The fruits of God's Word are blessings, life, and power to overcome Satan's influence. This is why it is so important to establish and maintain your relationship with Jesus Christ so you don't go back under Satan's control again.

How is it possible that a human being can use a gun or any weapon and kill human beings that they don't even know? And our society doesn't even recognize the influence that Satan had in the mind and heart of that individual. We can't see the truth because we have rejected the only One who can change a mind and heart from hate to love.

Revelation 3:17 describes the church in Laodicea as being blind. And in verse 18, the Holy Spirit advises them to buy ointment *"for your eyes so you will be able to see."*

I believe that the description of the church of Laodicea reflects the predominant church in America. We must always remember that the church is individuals and not a building. How in the world can you lead anyone to the Lord if you are spiritually blind?

We see evidence happening all around us that many professing Christians no longer believe in the truth of God's Word.

They have taken parts of the Word of God and declared that they don't apply to them in today's society. They say, "How can a loving God send anyone to hell?" They also believe in their hearts that they have more love and compassion for mankind than even God does.

I will declare to you that Satan has been effective with his lies in every aspect of our society today.

Probably the most important thing that you need to do is to examine yourself in light of the Holy Spirit's counsel to you. Will you listen and obey?

In our society today, what happens when anyone in authority and power espouses a desire to limit abortion? The spiritual battle intensifies against such an individual because Satan's number one goal is to kill God's creation and then to expand his power and control over the thinking of humanity through intimidation. So, Satan's objective is removing that person from power by any means. For example, Satan will use his human advocates who have a selfish desire to abort a baby and lead them on how to accomplish this goal. They will not stop! Since humanity is spiritually blind, they don't understand who is motivating them to accomplish this goal, which is Satan. We have been witnessing this happening in our society for a long time. How long will God allow this to happen?

How does God look at a woman telling him that her right to kill this baby supersedes God's right to give life to this baby and give this baby an opportunity to know Jesus Christ and accomplish their calling?

Are we witnessing Satan's human advocates displaying unprecedented rebellion against godly leaders and trying to remove them from power because they won't submit to their absolute goal to allow sin to flourish in every area of our lives and thinking? Are we witnessing other leaders coming to power who will conform to Satan's influence and obey his commands? Are we witnessing an intensified war against God and Christians? Is all of this occurring around the world? Does it seem like this anger and this hate toward God and Christians are growing day by day? Why do anger and hate affect every area in our society? This is a spiritual battle, and most of it can't be seen by the physical eye or understood with the natural mind. However, you are able to see the fruit of this anger and this hate through Satan's human advocates.

I believe Satan's next objective is to destroy God's blessing in the lives of all humanity. Consider what is going on in America today. America was founded on the phrase *In God We Trust.* We are witnessing the desire of Satan to destroy America. He will accomplish this goal through getting our eyes off God and putting our trust in the government for all our needs. That will destroy God's blessing upon this nation, and it will affect every nation in the world. I believe this is the generation in which Satan will be allowed to rule this world through the Antichrist. We will discuss more about this topic in the next chapter.

> *You should know this, Timothy, that in the last days there will be very difficult times. For people will love only themselves and their money. They will be boastful and proud, scoffing at God, disobedient to their parents, and ungrateful. They will consider nothing sacred. They will be unloving and unforgiving; they will slander others and have no self-control. They will be cruel and hate what is good. They will betray their friends, be reckless, be puffed up with pride, and love pleasure rather than God. They will act religious, but they will reject the power that could make them godly. Stay away from people like that!* (2 Timothy 3:1–5)

Satan's influence on individuals is revealed and displayed by their hate and their unforgiving spirit. We are witnessing the consequences of these actions toward others every day. Evil alters God's divine plan for your life. If you succumb to your own desire, which is motivated by Satan's influence, you will start seeing these characteristics in your life. In fact, evil has corrupted every area of our society. You witness the fruit of Satan's influence, and it is displayed before your eyes and ears every day. Do you recognize evil for what it is? And who is the author of all this evil? I believe rejecting the power that can make you godly will have eternal consequences.

The verses above describe the last-days society, which we are now living in. Please allow me to ask a few questions so you can decide who is influencing these actions (God, Satan, or yourself).

Who influences a person to only love themselves and their money?

- Who influences a person to be boastful and proud?
- Who influences a person to scoff at God in unbelief?
- Who influences a person to be disobedient to their parents and ungrateful?
- Who influences a person to consider nothing sacred?
- Who influences a person to be unloving and unforgiving?
- Who influences a person to slander others and have no self-control?
- Who influences a person to be cruel and to hate what is good?
- Who influences a person to betray their friends and be reckless?
- Who influences a person to be puffed up with pride?
- Who influences a person to love pleasure rather than God?
- Who influences a person to act religiously and then reject the power that could make them godly?

Then the passage gives us a stern warning to stay away from people like that. Why? Is it possible that if you hang around people like that, Satan will be able to influence you to act the same way?

This doesn't mean that you don't witness to those who display these characteristics, but you must recognize Satan's temptation for you is to compromise God's Word and for you to act just like them.

Your life of love for God and your obedience to his Word should be a witness to these people who display these characteristics. Allow the influence of the love of God to flow through you, so these people can see what godly character looks like.

Do you have an excuse not to do what God commands?

People already know the truth about Jesus Christ, but they refuse to believe that his power can change their actions so they could become holy. His power in you is the only way that you can overcome Satan's influence in the way you live your life.

The next verses declare that all humanity has already been given knowledge about God's law when they were created. There will be no excuse for their rebellion against God and for their unbelief.

> *Even Gentiles, who do not have God's written law, show that they know his law when they instinctively obey it, even without having heard it. They demonstrate that God's law is written in their hearts, for their own conscience and thoughts either accuse them or tell them they are doing right. And this is the message I proclaim—that the day is coming when God, through Christ Jesus, will judge everyone's secret life.* (Romans 2:14–16)

Again, you will decide who is influencing your actions: God, Satan, or yourself.

- Who influences a person to be unselfish?
- Who influences a person to be humble?
- Who influences a person to believe in God?
- Who influences a person to honor their parents and be grateful?
- Who influences a person to recognize the things that are sacred?
- Who influences a person to love and to be forgiving?
- Who influences a person to honor others and have self-control?
- Who influences a person to be kind and to love what is good?
- Who influences a person to be faithful to their friends and to be safe?
- Who influences a person to give praise to God instead of yourself?
- Who influences a person to love God more than loving pleasure?
- Who influences a person not to act religiously, but to seek the power that will make them godly?

Do you believe you can live a godly life? Please allow the Holy Spirit to perfect you and strengthen you so you can be like Jesus Christ. Do you desire in your heart and mind to become like Jesus Christ? Do you believe that you can possess all of the attributes above through the power of the Holy Spirit? Your answer will determine whether you seek after Jesus Christ or succumb to Satan's lies and influence.

This next verse destroys Satan's lie that you can't live a godly life.

> *For I can do everything through Christ, who gives me strength.* (Philippians 4:13)

You must believe in the power of Jesus Christ. The only power that can help you live a godly life is through Jesus Christ. Since this power comes from Jesus Christ, you can't take credit for what you accomplish! You must not allow pride to come between you and your Lord and Master, Jesus Christ.

The next passage describes our current generation!

> *For a time is coming when people will no longer listen to sound and wholesome teaching. They will follow their own desires and will look for teachers who will tell them whatever their itching ears want to hear. They will reject the truth and chase after myths.* (2 Timothy 4:3–4)

There are three spiritual influences that you can choose to follow to one degree or another. It is God's influence, Satan's influence, or your own. You will make the decision as to which path you will take. If you choose your own desire or Satan's influence, the end result is your destruction.

It is amazing to me how many preachers and teachers will compromise the truth of God's Word to have a greater following and to receive more money. Yet the problem is, carnal Christians don't want to hear the truth of God's Word.

Do you have a desire to find a more favorable teacher or pastor, and what spirit is motivating you to make that change? It is important that you allow the Holy Spirit and the Word of God to direct your path!

Have you witnessed this occurring in our society today? How many really rely on the Word of God for their truth? Where do myths come from? They come from people who are inspired or influenced by Satan and his advocates. What a dangerous time we live in and how easy it is to compromise on the Word of God. Please, establish the Word of God as the only truth to believe! You are the only one who can make that decision for your life.

> *Since they thought it foolish to acknowledge God, he abandoned them to their foolish thinking and let them do things that should never be done. Their lives became full of every kind of wickedness, sin, greed, hate, envy, murder, quarreling, deception, malicious behavior, and gossip. They are backstabbers, haters of God, insolent, proud, and boastful. They invent new ways of sinning, and they disobey their parents. They refuse to understand, break their promises, are heartless, and have no mercy. They know God's justice requires that those who do these things deserve to die, yet they do them anyway. Worse yet, they encourage others to do them, too.* (Romans 1:28–32)

I believe God has abandoned many in our society today, and that number is growing day by day. This dispensation of time is running out. God will proceed to the next phase of his plan in the near future. Will you be caught sleeping and unaware? How can anyone who lives in this society deny the truthfulness of these verses as they apply to our generation?

What does this passage mean? It means that, worse yet, those who do ungodly things encourage others to do them as well. You don't want to be found guilty of encouraging others to sin; this is a dangerous area, and judgment is certain. I believe this action or fruit adds additional consequences to your judgment. Only speak the truth of God's Word, and don't deviate from it.

So, let's consider, once again, John 8:44:

> *"He was a murderer from the beginning. He has always hated the truth, because there is no truth in him. When he lies, it is consistent with his character; for he is a liar and the father of lies."*

Since Lucifer is the father of lies, let us consider who actually planted these lies in the human mind. Just to name a few:

- Who planted the lie of evolution? Who planted the lie that life doesn't begin in the womb?
- Who planted the lies that there are many gods and religions and ways to serve God?

• Who planted the lie that the Word of God is not true?

All of these lies undermine the truth of God's Holy Word, and Satan is the father of these lies and so many more!

In today's society, lying has become a specialized art form, and it occurs in every area of life. Satan's ability to influence the minds of carnal human beings is beyond our understanding. A large part of our society no longer regards lying as evil and has accepted lying or twisting the truth as a necessary part of achieving their goal in life. You have witnessed many of our government officials establish as their character dishonesty and the inability to tell the truth. However, humanity has believed the lies of these officials and has supported them financially to help accomplish their goal. Lying has become an accepted reality to achieve their goal of power.

Have you accepted lying as a necessary part of achieving your goals or objectives? Do you recognize who is influencing you to lie?

God has never lied to humanity. He has given us the truth of his Word, and we will either believe his Word or believe Satan's lies. Your decision will have eternal consequences. You must always recognize that Satan's objective is to get human beings to deny or alter the absolute truth of the Word of God, and you have witnessed that going on for a long time from Satan's human advocates.

In God's new kingdom, lying will not become a form of communication. If you want to understand how God looks at lying, consider reading God's Word, because it declares all liars will be in hell forever.

Many in our society today describe the ideas that are changing our thinking and the way we live and act as a culture war. I prefer to describe it as evil (Satan's influence) versus good (God's influence). There is no question that our society today has chosen to believe Satan's lies.

So, is there any hope for our generation?

> *"Then if my people who are called by my name will humble themselves and pray and seek my face and turn from their wicked ways, I will hear from heaven and will forgive their sins and restore their land."* (2 Chronicles 7:14)

This verse makes a statement about what God requires from his people if they want to change the situation because of their past disobedience. The problem is that God's people have believed Satan's lies and are living wicked lives.

God establishes what is required if he is going to restore their land. First, they must humble themselves and recognize that God is their source of power, and not themselves. Second, they must seek "my face" (God's) in true repentance and stop sinning.

Nothing will change unless these actions of obedience are done before a holy God; these actions of obedience allow God to forgive their sins.

Will God's people in our generation realize they desperately need to repent so that God can restore our land? I have to admit, I see no evidence of that happening as it relates to God's people as a whole. I believe many people who claim to be his people have come to believe it is not necessary to repent and stop sinning because they are saved by grace and they are safe.

Again, you will decide if this verse applies to you and our generation.

I believe our society and generation are in a desperate situation. We have no desire to seek God, who is the only power that can restore and heal our hearts and minds from Satan's lies.

Let's describe just some of the spiritual conditions of our society today, but there are many more.

> *"Sin will be rampant everywhere, and the love of many will grow cold."* (Matthew 24:12)

The first part of this verse states that sin will be rampant throughout all of humanity. Then the second part describes a major problem in the church. You are a witness to the power of sin, and it has overpowered many in the church. The reason that many professing Christians are sinning is because they have allowed their love for God to grow cold. Their love grows chilly, slowly over time. They love their old lifestyle and have turned their backs on the only power that can set them free. They are spiritually blind and do not recognize their spiritual condition. They have also stopped obeying the counsel of the Holy Spirit. Is there any hope for this world if Christians have lost their first love in Jesus Christ?

> *"But the one who endures to the end will be saved."* (Matthew 24:13)

Always recognize that Satan and his advocates are at war with you and hate the spirit of Jesus Christ that lives in you. Will you succumb to their deception or endure to the end by living a godly life? If you stumble and fall, the Holy Spirit will convict you of your sin, and then it is your responsibility to repent of your sin. Then God is faithful to forgive you of your sin. You are learning and being perfected in becoming an obedient servant of the Most High God. Endure to the end! God is not finished with you yet; as long as you live in your physical body, he is giving you the opportunity to repent and depend on him.

This next verse describes another phase or event in God's plan:

> *"But when the Son of Man returns, how many will he find on the earth who have faith?"* (Luke 18:8)

I believe this verse describes two different time frames. First, when Jesus Christ returns in the clouds to catch away the body of Christ. Second, when Jesus Christ returns to this earth in his physical body at the end of the seven-year tribulation to set up his rule on this earth for one thousand years. This verse asks an important question: How many will he find on this earth who have faith in him?

I believe that this verse implies that many (compared to the total population) will not have faith in Jesus Christ.

What are the consequences of unbelief? Human beings have been rejecting the truth about God for a long time. Yet they don't even recognize where the lie they are believing is coming from: Satan and his advocates. Humanity has believed this lie for so long that they no longer even believe that Satan exists.

Satan doesn't care, and that is part of his strategy. His only objective is to destroy God's creation: you. The fact is, Satan has no love for you or any human being, now or ever.

What will you do with the time you have left on this earth? Do you know who motivates you to do the things you do? Your actions identify who you are serving. Are you serving Jesus Christ and obeying his Word? Are you actually serving Satan and working to accomplish his goals? God has given you free will, and you will choose which spiritual power you will obey. You need to examine yourself before it is too late.

If you have given your life to Jesus Christ, never forget he has given you power through the Holy Spirit to be an overcomer of Satan's influence.

If you know you're motivated by Satan's influence, reconsider your decision and turn to Jesus Christ, who will give you the power to overcome your real enemy, Satan.

Please don't give up. Finish the race in victory, through the power of the Holy Spirit, because of your love for Jesus Christ.

I believe this is the generation in which the next phase (tribulation) of God's plan will occur. It is because of our society's rebellion against believing in Jesus Christ and refusing to obey his laws and commands. This unbelief in Jesus Christ and God produces an attitude of having no fear of God's judgment on them. The consequences of this attitude mean that God must change his approach on reaching humanity.

22

A Major Change Occurs: How God Reaches Souls for His Kingdom Through Tribulation

This chapter will not be an in-depth study of the seven-year tribulation. I will give you highlights of events that will occur and explain what will happen, perhaps from a different perspective. However, God gave us insight into this part of his plan, but mystery still remains concerning how it will all happen in real life. This is my understanding of Scripture as it relates to the time frame surrounding the tribulation period. The purpose of prophecy is to *"give a clear witness for Jesus,"* as in Revelation 19:10.

I believe the following verse identifies the time frame we are discussing.

> *"But you, Daniel, keep this prophecy a secret; seal up the book until the time of the end, when many will rush here and there, and knowledge will increase."* (Daniel 12:4)

This verse identifies a time frame (the end) that is different from any time before. It identifies a society that has transportation options, which allow them to rush here and there. Our transportation options are greater than any generation's since the beginning of time.

The next characteristic of the last generation before the appearance of the Antichrist is their great knowledge—the verse says that knowledge will increase.

Just to give you one statistic, the sum total of human knowledge doubles every twelve months or so.[1]

We are living in the last generation before the Antichrist is revealed. The verses below give us more evidence of the time we are living in.

Another reason for God's decision on how to deal with humanity is found in the next verse:

> *"For her sins are piled as high as heaven, and God remembers her evil deeds."* (Revelation 18:5)

Humanity has reached a point in their love for sin and obedience to Satan's influence where it becomes necessary for God to change his approach to how to win the lost.

The next part of God's plan is the catching away of the bride of Christ, those who are victorious over Satan and their own free will through the power of Jesus Christ.

> *"Keep alert at all times. And pray that you might be strong enough to escape these coming horrors and stand before the Son of Man."* (Luke 21:36)

This verse indicates that the body of Jesus Christ is removed from this earth because they are strong enough in the power of Jesus Christ, and he has determined he is not going to allow them to suffer punishment as a result of his command.

> *Don't be fooled by what they say. For that day will not come until there is a great rebellion against God and the man of lawlessness is revealed—the one who brings destruction.* (2 Thessalonians 2:3)

This verse gives a warning that many will be fooled when the next phase of God's plan will occur. Because of the rebellion of humanity against God, the next phase of God's plan is to remove the body of Christ (the church) from this earth. That removal will bring chaos, and peace will be taken from the earth, and

[1]Vincent Lassalle, *Bridge Builders: Learning from Those Ushering the Future of Society* (n.p.: Librinova, 2018), sec. 3.2.

that will allow Satan through the Antichrist to begin the process of establishing his rule and form his kingdom, or revised Rome.

The first sign for all to witness is the great rebellion against God. How can anyone deny that rebellion against God isn't occurring right now? Not only is it occurring now, but it is growing stronger day by day. Evil (Satan's influence) is manifested in the actions of so many in our society today. There is a concerted effort among Satan's human advocates to deny God and Jesus Christ. They tell you that you don't have to live by God's law or obey his commands—what a lie! This rebellion comes from humanity, which has a carnal mind, and they are obeying Satan's influence or temptation to do evil. This great rebellion against God is occurring now and will continue to grow before and until the Antichrist is revealed.

The Antichrist will rule in the area of the old Roman empire. Of the ten kingdoms (referred to in Daniel 7:24), the Antichrist will rule one of them. The Antichrist will have to conquer three of the kingdoms and the other six kingdoms will submit to his leadership to form this new kingdom and become a world power. To form this kingdom, the Antichrist will kill millions and bring great destruction to the world. I don't know how long it will take for the Antichrist to form this new kingdom.

I believe humanity's hatred for God (in this time frame) is the reason God allows Satan to establish his kingdom, and it is to reveal Satan's true intentions toward the Jews (God's chosen people) and all of humanity that is under his absolute control. I also believe God wants all humanity to physically see and witness what the consequences would be for Satan to rule humanity. Also, God has removed the mask, so to speak, and has given mankind a clear choice concerning which one they are going to serve and worship, God or Satan. The destruction that occurs during this time frame is a result of Satan's desire to be god.

This rebellion against God that we are witnessing right now—is it the last rebellion before the Antichrist is revealed?

Let's discuss highlights of the changes that will occur that prove that God changes the way he deals with humanity. We have been beneficiaries of God's mercy, but now it changes into God's judgment. It is a sad reality that most of humanity will not serve Jesus Christ during the time of mercy. They will not control their free will through the power of the Holy Spirit and obey his laws.

They must now witness Satan's true motive, and that is to destroy all of humanity who don't completely reject Jesus Christ. During this time frame, those who are going to be saved must reject Satan as their god and as a consequence will have to suffer many afflictions, including death by beheading.

The analysis of the Scriptures below will give us evidence of the serious changes that will occur. I will break this information down into major events that will occur before the beginning of the seven-year tribulation—major events that will occur in the first three and a half years, and events that will occur at mid-tribulation. Then we will discuss major events that will happen during the last three and a half years.

The ministry of the church is no longer mentioned as a tool that God uses to reach the lost during the tribulation.

Some Major Events That Will Occur Before the Seven-Year Tribulation

God reveals the first evidence of how he is going to change the hearts and minds of those rebellious souls who are going to accept Jesus Christ as their Savior.

> *"Wait! Don't harm the land or the sea or the trees until we have placed the seal of God on the foreheads of his servants." And I heard how many were marked with the seal of God—144,000 were sealed from all the tribes of Israel.* (Revelation 7:3–4)

These verses identify who the 144,000 are, and they are from the twelve tribes of Israel—12,000 each.

They are identified as servants, and they have the seal of God on their foreheads. Everyone will be able to physically see the seal of God on their foreheads. When the seven seal and trumpet judgments occur, humans are able to witness that none of the 144,000 are affected by these events or harmed by any of the judgments. It is during this time frame that one-fourth of all humanity will be killed by the sword and famine and disease and wild animals.

When the church was on this earth, they were known as servants of God and Jesus Christ. What does it mean that the 144,000 are servants of God? I believe it means they tell the truth to the rebellious people of this world about Jesus Christ and why these judgments are happening to them. They will tell the people of this earth what they are told to say. Revelation 14:4–5 describes the 144,000 in this way:

> *They have kept themselves as pure as virgins, following the Lamb wherever he goes. They have been purchased from among the people on the earth as a special offering to God and to the Lamb. They have told no lies; they are without blame.*

These verses state that the Lamb goes before them, and they never tell a lie or alter the truth. Also, they never worship any other gods. They stay faithful to God and Jesus Christ in everything they do and say.

The next thing I want to discuss is that the 144,000 are Jews. When Jesus Christ came to this earth the first time, the Jews rejected him as their messiah. Now, these 144,000 won't reject Jesus Christ and will be his servants to proclaim the truth and do as he commands.

I believe their ministry will start before the covenant is signed between the Antichrist and Israel and will be completed at mid-tribulation. (We have already discussed the Antichrist establishing his kingdom before the seven-year tribulation.)

Some Important Events That Will Occur in the First Three and a Half Years

This period begins with the signing of the covenant between the Antichrist and Israel.

> *"The ruler will make a treaty with the people for a period of one set of seven."* (Daniel 9:27)

After Satan's kingdom is established through the Antichrist, the Antichrist will make a covenant with Israel for seven years. This covenant starts when the Jews sign the covenant with the Antichrist. Making this covenant with the Antichrist will come at a great cost to Israel.

Once again, they have put their trust in a man (the Antichrist) and not Jesus Christ.

During the first forty-two months, Satan's power is limited by God.

The next event that God reveals that will change many of the hearts and minds of the rebellious people is shown in the following verse:

> *"And I will give power to my two witnesses, and they will be clothed in burlap and will prophesy during those 1,260 days."* (Revelation 11:3)

After the signing of the covenant between the Antichrist and Israel, these two witnesses appear in Jerusalem.

These two witnesses declare that Jesus Christ is Lord and exercise their God-given authority to do miracles to prove that they are telling the truth. God has limited their ministry to 1,260 days. Neither the Antichrist nor Satan has the power to stop these two witnesses from telling the world about Jesus Christ.

I believe that these two witnesses will be able to reach the world with their message through the technology of the Internet. God has chosen this method to give mankind another opportunity to know the truth about him: that he is the only true God and not the one who will be revealed after the 1,260 days of the ministry of the two witnesses.

> *These two prophets are the two olive trees and the two lampstands that stand before the Lord of all the earth. If anyone tries to harm them, fire flashes from their mouths and consumes their enemies. This is how anyone who tries to harm them must die. They have power to shut the sky so that no rain will fall for as long as they prophesy. And they have the power to turn the rivers and oceans into blood, and to strike the earth with every kind of plague as often as they wish.* (Revelation 11:4–6)

God is going to clearly establish that he is the only true God, but each person will have to choose whom they are going to serve and obey. Now the evidence that is set before mankind is different from any other time in history, and they will have to decide whom they are going to believe, God or Satan. The two witnesses will proclaim and prove beyond any doubt that they have been given these powers by the God of this universe. The purpose is to establish before mankind what God requires from his creation and that they are not to serve any other gods. Satan has already set up his kingdom and has been limited in what he can do at this time.

The people who belong to this world will not serve the one and only true God, because they love their sin.

However, many will begin their journey in serving the one and only true God.

Again, God has chosen not to use the church as his witness to the lost during this time frame, because their ministry is complete.

Some Important Events That Will Occur Around Mid-Tribulation

A lot changes after the 1,260 days of ministry by the two witnesses and the ministry of the 144,000 Jews to the world. I believe the fruit of the ministry of the two witnesses and the 144,000 will be effective. Now comes the next phase of God's plan for mankind and what is going to be required of them to stay true to God and Jesus Christ.

> *"Therefore, rejoice, O heavens!*
> *And you who live in the heavens, rejoice!*
> *But terror will come on the earth and the sea,*
> *for the devil has come down to you in great anger,*
> *knowing that he has little time."* (Revelation 12:12)

I believe this event occurs just before the end of the 1,260 days of ministry of the two witnesses.

This verse reveals that Satan recognizes that God has given him (Satan) only a little time left to accomplish his goal—even though he still believes he's going to win. Also, Satan has just been cast out of heaven where he had been accusing brothers and sisters of Jesus Christ before God day and night. As a result of this event, Satan's anger intensifies against Israel and the new believers of Jesus Christ (the potential fruit of the two witnesses and the 144,000). I believe that Satan is cast down to earth and is no longer the prince and power of the air. Satan will have no power to stop or interfere with the angels completing the task they have been given to pour out God's judgment on the earth.

This event brings about major changes in how Satan deals

with mankind and how God purifies those who are going to stay true to God and Jesus Christ.

> *When they complete their testimony, the beast that comes up out of the bottomless pit will declare war against them, and he will conquer them and kill them. And their bodies will lie in the main street of Jerusalem, the city that is figuratively called "Sodom" and "Egypt," the city where their Lord was crucified. And for three and a half days, all peoples, tribes, languages, and nations will stare at their bodies. No one will be allowed to bury them. All the people who belong to this world will gloat over them and give presents to each other to celebrate the death of the two prophets who had tormented them.*
>
> *But after three and a half days, God breathed life into them, and they stood up! Terror struck all who were staring at them. Then a loud voice from heaven called to the two prophets, "Come up here!" And they rose to heaven in a cloud as their enemies watched.*
> (Revelation 11:7–12)

God will not allow Satan to kill the two witnesses through the Antichrist until after their ministry of 1,260 days is complete.

Once God breathes life back into the two witnesses, they and the 144,000 will be caught up to heaven because their ministry and work is complete.

The fact that the world is a witness to the two witnesses coming back to life and rising to heaven is a testimony to the world that God in heaven is the one and only true God to be worshipped.

It is at this time that the Antichrist will be allowed to do whatever he wants to do on this earth.

> *They worshiped the dragon for giving the beast such power, and they also worshiped the beast. "Who is as great as the beast?" they exclaimed. "Who is able to fight against him?"*
>
> *Then the beast was allowed to speak great blasphemies against God. And he was given authority to do whatever*

> *he wanted for forty-two months. And he spoke terrible words of blasphemy against God, slandering his name and his dwelling—that is, those who dwell in heaven. And the beast was allowed to wage war against God's holy people and to conquer them. And he was given authority to rule over every tribe and people and language and nation.* (Revelation 13:4–7)

This time frame is the last forty-two months of the original seven-year period. It is at this time the Antichrist/Satan breaks the covenant with the Jews. He goes into the temple of the Jews and desecrates it and claims to be God. Then he starts a war with the Jewish people. His desire is to destroy and conquer them because of his hate for God and all he stands for.

Why does God allow the Antichrist to blaspheme God and wage war against his holy people?

During the first forty-two months, I believe God has made himself known to humanity through the ministry of the two witnesses and the 144,000 Jews, and a great number of mankind will begin their journey in believing in Jesus Christ.

I believe we will find the answer in the following verses:

> *Anyone with ears to hear*
> *should listen and understand.*
> *Anyone who is destined for prison*
> *will be taken to prison.*
> *Anyone destined to die by the sword*
> *will die by the sword.*
>
> *This means that God's holy people must endure persecution patiently and remain faithful.*
> (Revelation 13:9–10)

I believe that these people who have begun their journey must be tested and tried and be given the opportunity to change their minds because they have free will to choose whom they are going to serve, God or Satan. This time frame is compacted to be not more than three and a half years.

Satan will tempt God's holy people through the Antichrist and the false prophet. All they have to do is take the mark of the beast and they will be allowed to live, or not go to prison. Only those who actually endure persecution patiently and remain faithful are God's holy people.

Let's consider another verse:

> *And they have defeated him by the blood of the Lamb*
> *and by their testimony.*
> *And they did not love their lives so much*
> *that they were afraid to die.* (Revelation 12:11)

Only those who refuse to take the mark of the beast and are willing to be killed will be successful in defeating Satan. They will be able to follow through with their decision to give up their physical life because of the blood of Jesus Christ. This decision to give up their life will establish their testimony to the world that it is better to obey God than it is to live in this world without him. They will overcome their free will to live.

Would you stay faithful to Jesus Christ, or would you love your life so much that you would give up serving Jesus Christ to continue to live in your physical body? I believe you are making that decision for yourself, and you probably don't realize the seriousness of your decision. It is your actions in life that reveal your true decision and your love for God.

The following verses establish Satan's objective to seal mankind's judgment so they will be forever separated from God's love:

> *Then I saw another beast come up out of the earth. He had two horns like those of a lamb, but he spoke with the voice of a dragon. He exercised all the authority of the first beast. And he required all the earth and its people to worship the first beast, whose fatal wound had been healed. He did astounding miracles, even making fire flash down to earth from the sky while everyone was watching. And with all the miracles he was allowed to perform on behalf of the first beast, he deceived all the people who belong to this world. He ordered the people to make a great statue of the first beast, who was fatally wounded and then came back to life. He was then*

> *permitted to give life to this statue so that it could speak. Then the statue of the beast commanded that anyone refusing to worship it must die.*
>
> *He required everyone—small and great, rich and poor, free and slave—to be given a mark on the right hand or on the forehead. And no one could buy or sell anything without that mark, which was either the name of the beast or the number representing his name.* (Revelation 13:11–17)

I believe Satan copies God's method of identifying his own so the world can see who has given their allegiance to him (Satan). Anyone who takes the mark of the beast will have condemned themselves to everlasting punishment. The difference is Satan has no ability to protect them from God's wrath on those who have received Satan's mark. God allows Satan to do many miracles so that mankind can recognize it is not about miracles but obedience to God, their Creator.

Since the two witnesses and the 144,000 are already in heaven by this point in Scripture, how will God give mankind the truth of who to serve?

> *And I saw another angel flying through the sky, carrying the eternal Good News to proclaim to the people who belong to this world—to every nation, tribe, language, and people. "Fear God," he shouted. "Give glory to him. For the time has come when he will sit as judge. Worship him who made the heavens, the earth, the sea, and all the springs of water."* (Revelation 14:6–7)

Satan has no power to stop this angel from doing what God commanded him to do. These verses give no length of time for this ministry to be complete. Is it possible that it will last around 1,260 days?

Through this angel, God will make it clear to mankind who they should worship, Jesus Christ. Now mankind will have to choose what is more important: life, food, buying, selling, or giving it all up to serve the only true God.

> *"And the Good News about the Kingdom will be preached throughout the whole world, so that all nations will hear it; and then the end will come."* (Matthew 24:14)

I believe it is the angel in Revelation 14:6–7 that will actually accomplish God's command to preach to all the nations so they will hear it. (It is not the church.) The days will not be shortened until the angel completes this task.

I believe the physical return of Jesus Christ is imminent when this angel completes his task.

> *Then a third angel followed them, shouting, "Anyone who worships the beast and his statue or who accepts his mark on the forehead or on the hand must drink the wine of God's anger. It has been poured full strength into God's cup of wrath. And they will be tormented with fire and burning sulfur in the presence of the holy angels and the Lamb. The smoke of their torment will rise forever and ever, and they will have no relief day or night, for they have worshiped the beast and his statue and have accepted the mark of his name."*
> (Revelation 14:9–11)

I believe this angel's ministry is the same length of time as the ministry of the first angel who proclaims the good news. There is no question that God will reveal the truth to mankind about whom they should serve. He will also declare the consequences for their rebellion and disobedience. Mankind will never be able to say, "I didn't know."

> *This means that God's holy people must endure persecution patiently, obeying his commands and maintaining their faith in Jesus.* (Revelation 14:12)

Do you realize the privilege we have now to freely serve Jesus Christ before mankind turns their backs on him? Whom will you serve, worship, and obey? Serve, worship, and obey Jesus Christ now, in this time of mercy!

The fact is, during the time of the end, God's holy people

will have to go through difficult trials but will remain steadfast in their obedience to Jesus Christ.

> *But the people who did not die in these plagues still refused to repent of their evil deeds and turn to God. They continued to worship demons and idols made of gold, silver, bronze, stone, and wood—idols that can neither see nor hear nor walk! And they did not repent of their murders or their witchcraft or their sexual immorality or their thefts.* (Revelation 9:20–21)

This passage shows that the ungodly will love the sins that Satan entices them to commit and will refuse to give them up to serve and obey Jesus Christ. In Satan's kingdom, his only objective is to separate you from your Creator. Satan doesn't do it because he loves mankind.

It amazes me that the people of this world will serve Satan because he allows them to exercise their free will and do evil deeds. Numerous times in Revelation, God reveals himself through judgments, and people of this world recognize where these judgments are coming from. Yet they refuse to repent, all because they love evil, even when God executes judgment on them, trying to convince them to change their minds and accept his ways and turn away from Satan's path. The people of this world (Satan's captives) will refuse to believe in Jesus Christ and obey his laws. They will instead love their freedom to sin and do what is evil.

Free will in a person's life can't be controlled without the power and love of Jesus Christ in them. We can see this truth even today, in our society. America is on its way to destruction. The fact is, mankind desires to break God's commands because they want no boundaries or limitations in what they think or do, and if that is not controlled by the power of Jesus Christ, no kingdom can last.

God is revealing and proving to all his creation that accepting God's authority and loving him and exercising obedience to all his commands and laws is the only way his kingdom can survive throughout eternity. That is why God's creation must be tested and tried.

> *"In fact, unless that time of calamity is shortened, not a single person will survive. But it will be shortened for the sake of God's chosen ones."* (Matthew 24:22)

God's chosen ones are actually a remnant of the Jewish people. Ever since the Antichrist desecrated the temple in the middle of the tribulation, the Antichrist's objective (along with Satan's) was to completely kill all the Jews. God will not allow that to happen because the Jewish remnant has an important responsibility to fulfill in the thousand-year reign of Jesus Christ.

God determines the day that Jesus Christ will physically return to set up his kingdom.

> *Then I saw heaven opened, and a white horse was standing there. Its rider was named Faithful and True, for he judges fairly and wages a righteous war. His eyes were like flames of fire, and on his head were many crowns. A name was written on him that no one understood except himself. He wore a robe dipped in blood, and his title was the Word of God. The armies of heaven, dressed in the finest of pure white linen, followed him on white horses. From his mouth came a sharp sword to strike down the nations. He will rule them with an iron rod. He will release the fierce wrath of God, the Almighty, like juice flowing from a winepress. On his robe at his thigh was written this title: King of all kings and Lord of all lords.* (Revelation 19:11–16)

Here are some of the highlights from these verses.

Jesus Christ is the rider on the white horse, leading his army of redeemed saints, coming to fulfill God's plan that was prophesied long ago.

The armies of heaven don't have to fight; Jesus Christ does everything himself through his spoken Word. Satan and his armies do not have a chance; they can do nothing to accomplish their goal of stopping Jesus Christ from taking his rightful place as King of kings and Lord of lords.

Jesus Christ also executes God's wrath on those who took the mark of the beast and worshipped Satan. This should give us a clear understanding of how God looks at his creation who believe in other gods and not the true living God. The eternal fate of those who will not believe in Jesus Christ (now) will be no different from the fate of those who take the mark of the beast.

Everyone living at this time will be able to physically see Jesus Christ in all his glory, and no one will be able to touch him or have the power to alter any prophecy he has come to fulfill.

Are you one of the people who believe that if you miss the catching away of the church (during the time of mercy), you will be able to serve Jesus Christ in the tribulation? Why would you even consider that as a desirable option? Why wouldn't you consider now as the time to give your heart and life to Jesus Christ? Why wait?

> *Then I saw the beast and the kings of the world and their armies gathered together to fight against the one sitting on the horse and his army. And the beast was captured, and with him the false prophet who did mighty miracles on behalf of the beast—miracles that deceived all who had accepted the mark of the beast and who worshiped his statue. Both the beast and his false prophet were thrown alive into the fiery lake of burning sulfur. Their entire army was killed by the sharp sword that came from the mouth of the one riding the white horse. And the vultures all gorged themselves on the dead bodies.* (Revelation 19:19–21)

Satan inspires the Antichrist and the kings of the world to believe they can defeat and conquer Jesus Christ and the redeemed and stop prophecy from being fulfilled.

Not only are the Antichrist and the kings of this world deceived, but Satan has deceived himself into believing his own lie that he can overthrow the King of kings through his army.

What is *prophecy*? Prophecy is God's ability to know the future before it happens. Knowing the future before it happens is one of God's attributes that makes him God and like no one else. And God has given us the Word of God as evidence to help us to decide to worship him and no one else. Throughout all of time, God has been revealing himself to the creation that he created. So, all of prophecy must be fulfilled or God isn't all-knowing!

I pray that this book has revealed more about God's plan and love for you.

Will you love him with all your heart, mind, and soul?

May God bless you as you grow closer to him and understand the importance of obeying God in everything you do and say. The outcome of your decision will last forever, and it will be final.

After all this begins a new phase of God's plan. That is, the thousand-year reign of Jesus Christ along with the redeemed, which I have already covered in an earlier chapter.

I believe this completes the message that the Holy Spirit wanted me to share with you.

I pray that you will examine yourself in light of the Holy Spirit's counsel and the Word of God!

23

My Testimony!

First, I want to give thanks to my Creator for what he has taught me. The insight that the Holy Spirit has given me will last forever. And yet, there is so much more to learn. I pray that the Holy Spirit will continue to give me wisdom and understanding of the Word of God! My life and understanding of the Word of God will never be the same. My spiritual eyes have been opened to see things differently in this physical world. The spiritual battle that is raging today will end one day, and my desire is to hear my Lord and Savior say to me, "Enter into my kingdom, you good and faithful servant."

After writing this book, which I believe was inspired by the Holy Spirit, my prayer and hope for you is that you will be inspired to read the Word of God and allow the Holy Spirit to give you divine revelation of his truth.

When the Holy Spirit led me to write this book, I wondered, *Why me?* I want to reemphasize the importance of the Word of God and how it empowers us to live a holy life. The Word of God is the only authority that all humanity should put their trust in and establish it in their hearts and minds and know that the Word of God is the truth. We all will be judged by the Word of God, and none of God's creation will escape this examination. The outcome of this judgment will be forever and ever. What is the love of your life?

For God to desire the love and fellowship of this creation, humanity, who was created in his image and likeness, is amazing to me. I am only beginning to understand why God views those who submit to his authority and who will obey him as jewels and pillars in his new kingdom. Only those who love God and submit to his authority will ever be able to control their free will and enter this new kingdom. This is accomplished because they believe in Jesus Christ and rely on his power to overcome their free will.

I believe this relationship that God has with those who freely submit to his authority is different from any other relationship he has with any other creation he has ever created.

I want to be and do everything that God created me to do, especially throughout eternity. There is so much more that has been prepared for me that I do not understand. Yet I believe my love for God will continue to grow and my worship of him will never end.

I give God all the glory for the truth that I have been given, and I pray that I have shared with you divine revelation that will be a blessing to you and help you to be the overcomer that God wants you to be.

About the Author

Roy Chaney was born into a Christian family. Later, his parents had three more sons. He married his wife, Sharon, and they had been married for over fifty-two years when Sharon passed away on November 11, 2019. The couple tried to have children, but it looked like they would not be able to conceive. One Sunday morning, their pastor asked anyone wanting children to come up front to pray to God for his blessing on their family. They were prayed for, and about ten months later, Sharon gave birth to a baby girl. They had already been married for five years, so they knew it was a miracle. Their son did not come for another seven years and after a lot of prayer. Another miracle. They were blessed to have five grandchildren.

Roy served as an army medic in Vietnam and witnessed the consequences of Satan's influence on mankind. So many died around him, and he knew God had spared him.

Following his military service, he retired from a newspaper after forty-two years. For most of his adult life, he has been a Sunday school teacher. The Holy Spirit gave Roy an understanding of God's plan to build his kingdom.

Today, Roy resides in Colorado Springs, where he is active in his church and enjoys spending time with his family.

Notes

Notes

Notes

Notes